Reflective Practice and Supervision for Coaches

Coaching in Practice series

The aim of this series is to help coaching professionals gain a broader understanding of the challenges and issues they face in coaching, enabling them to make the leap from being a 'good-enough' coach to an outstanding one. This series is an essential aid for both the novice coach eager to learn how to grow a coaching practice, and the more experienced coach looking for new knowledge and strategies. Combining theory with practice, it provides a comprehensive guide to becoming successful in this rapidly expanding profession.

Forthcoming titles:

Hayes: *NLP Coaching*
Bluckert: *Psychological Dimensions to Coaching*
Vaughan Smith: *Therapist into Coach*

Reflective Practice and Supervision for Coaches

Julie Hay

Open University Press

Open University Press
McGraw-Hill Education
McGraw-Hill House
Shoppenhangers Road
Maidenhead
Berkshire
England
SL6 2QL

email: enquiries@openup.co.uk
world wide web: www.openup.co.uk

and Two Penn Plaza, New York, NY 10121-2289, USA

First published 2007

Copyright © Julie Hay 2007

A catalogue record of this book is available from the British Library

ISBN-10: 0 335 22063 0 (pb) 0 335 22064 9 (hb)
ISBN-13: 978 0335 22063 2 (pb) 978 0335 22064 9 (hb)

Library of Congress Cataloging-in-Publication Data
CIP data applied for

Typeset by YHT Ltd, London
Printed in Poland by OZGraf S.A.
www.polskabook.pl

The **McGraw·Hill** Companies

Contents

List of Activities

List of Figures

Series Preface

The coaching world is expanding. A profession that was largely unknown a decade ago is now an attractive second career for increasing numbers of people looking for new ways of growing their interest in the development of people. Some observers reckon that the number of new coaches joining the market is doubling every year.

Yet while there are many books which cater for the beginner coach, including my own book, also published by Open University Press, *Coaching Skills: A Handbook*, there are relatively few which explore and deepen more specialist aspects of the role. That is the purpose of this series. It is called *Coaching in Practice* because the aim is to unite theory and practice in an accessible way. The books are short, designed to be easily understood without in any way compromising on the integrity of the ideas they explore. All are written by senior coaches with, in every case, many years of hands-on experience.

This series is for you if you are undertaking or completing your coaching training and perhaps in the early stages of the unpredictability, pleasures and dilemmas that working with actual clients brings. Now that you have passed the honeymoon stage, you may have begun to notice the limitations of your approaches and knowledge. You are eager for more information and guidance. You probably know that it is hard to make the leap between being a good-enough coach and an outstanding one. You are thirsty for more help and challenge. You may also be one of the many people still contemplating a career in coaching. If so, these books will give you useful direction on many of the issues which preoccupy, perplex and delight the working coach.

That is where I hope you will find the *Coaching in Practice* series so useful.

Other titles in this series are about hands-on work with clients. This one is about the equally important topic of how you build a coaching business. Being a coach means that you are in effect running a small business, but what does this mean in practice? How is the coaching market developing and what are the implications for any coach? How should you sustain yourself while you are building your business? Which promotional activities really pay off and which are waste of time and money? Coaching programmes are typically short and finite so it is essential to have a steady stream of new clients, but how do you find them, and even more importantly, how do you sell with integrity? This book aims to give you practical guidance on all of these topics—and more, from someone who has been there and done it.

No coach in the fiercely competitive market in which we now work can afford to ignore the need for supervision and reflection. Discussing and thinking about your work with a more experienced coach can be a wonderfully stretching, challenging and liberating experience, but the question is how do you do it? How do you get the most out of a supervisor? How do you reflect on your current practice with a colleague? Julie Hay is one of the UK's most experienced coaches and supervisors with a depth of understanding that few can rival. The questions she raises and the activities she suggests in this book are wise, thought-provoking, practical and enjoyable. In the end, it's about improvement, a never-ending quest for those of us working in this developing profession.

About this Book

My target audience

I've written this book with coaches in mind, with the intention of helping you to get the maximum benefit from reflecting on your practice. I've explained how you can do this alone, with colleagues, and with a supervisor. It is not a book about how to do coaching but about how to review what you've done and keep on improving.

By coach, I mean anyone who works professionally in ways that help other people to grow and develop. I will explain this is more detail in Chapter 1 – for now, let me just say that I think reflection and supervision are valuable whether you are a full-time coach or a line manager who does some coaching or mentoring alongside your more general managerial duties.

By formal supervisor, I mean someone whose function is to assist you in reflecting on your practice. I do not mean the type of supervisor who is a first-line manager or team leader with responsibility for making sure you do your job properly. Instead, I am writing about the type of supervision that has been common in social work and therapy circles for many years, where the focus is on reviewing your practice in order to increase your self-awareness and hence your competence. The value of this form of supervision is increasingly being recognized wherever coaching takes place.

I am assuming that you will have some experience of coaching and hence some knowledge of some of the theoretical models that apply. However, because there are so many theories and frameworks, I will not assume that you know the same theories that I know. Instead, I'll give some brief explanations plus references – feel free to skip through these parts and go straight to the activities when you already know the material.

The structure of the book

This book is divided into three main sections, plus this short introduction and an equally short closing piece. The first three chapters focus on what to do. Chapter 1 begins by inviting you to consider what reflection and supervision are, as well as inviting you to position your practice so you can decide which reflection and supervision formats will best fit your practice. Chapter 2 is on ways of reflecting so as to maximize your learning, followed by Chapter 3 that presents a range of ideas relating to reflecting with others, whether they be peers or a formal supervisor.

The second section is about what to pay attention to. Again, this consists of three chapters and these contain three options for your reflection and supervision processes – whether to base it on the stages of the coaching; or to pay attention to the processes that occur between coach and client and also between supervisee and supervisor; or to process systemically through a range of contexts, people, interactions and dynamics.

The third section adds some general considerations that will increase your level of awareness about what is going on and provide you with frameworks for generating more options. Chapter 7 is on contracting – get this right and everything that follows functions better; Chapter 8 covers psychological models that you can use to analyse what is really going on; and Chapter 9 is about working cross-culturally.

Finally, I've ended with a short 'what next' piece that prompts you to go beyond the various activities that are spread throughout the book and think about your priorities and longer-term plans relating to reflection and supervision.

The theories

In terms of the theories I will quote, let me warn you that I am somewhat biased. I am internationally accredited as a transactional analysis (TA) trainer and supervisor in organizational and educational applications and internationally licensed as a trainer of neuro-linguistic programming (NLP). Many of the theories I offer will therefore come from these two approaches, which I think work even better when combined with each other. I am not expecting that you will already know a lot about either TA or NLP, although you will probably recognize some of the concepts.

In the hope that you like what you read, I will give references so that you can do further reading in terms of how these might be more generally useful in your work as a coach, because I am writing here about how you reflect rather than how you practise. Over the many years that TA and NLP have been developing, both approaches have borrowed concepts from other approaches and some of the original attributions have become lost over time. The references I give may not, therefore, be to the originator of a concept but to the author who first applied a specific concept within the TA or NLP field, or in some cases to the author (including me) who has provided a particularly relevant explication.

Lest you don't much like reading about theories, keep in mind that it is hard to reflect without them. We need language to know what we are thinking and theories provide us with labels for constructs that we can hold in our minds. Although the theories themselves are abstract thoughts, often arrived at via conjecture, they can be used to explain phenomena – in other words, they're helpful in working out what's been going on. We also need language so we can communicate. If you take your car in for service, you may be confused when the mechanic tells you what is required in very technical terms that mean nothing to you. We need shared labels to understand what we are saying to each other and theoretical frameworks provide these.

The activities

There are a number of suggested activities scattered throughout the book. They are of course designed to help you reflect and to get the maximum benefit from supervision. If you don't think about what you're doing, you're unlikely to identify options for improvement.

You do not have to do all of the activities, nor do you have to work through them in the order in which they appear in the book. They are intended as a resource for you, to choose the ones which seem most relevant. Your choices may change over time, and that in itself might also become a matter for you to reflect upon.

Keep in mind that you can vary the activities to suit your own needs – they are only suggestions and not rules.

A glossary has been provided, and the first occurrence of the terms in the glossary is highlighted in bold.

A final comment

Finally, let me explain why there are a number of acronyms, alliterations and other gimmicks scattered through this book. These are *donkey bridges* (Townsend 1994) – a translation of a term used by German trainers as a metaphor for coaxing students into the greener pastures that become available to them as they learn. I use them because they help most people remember more material more readily. With a donkey bridge to help you recall the key headings, you are free to concentrate on the content and process of your reflection and supervision sessions.

Except where you may be working together through one of the activities, it can break the connection with colleagues or supervisor if you have to keep referring to the book or your notes. It can be even more of an impediment if you need to look at a checklist once you start reflecting during your work with clients. For this, you need simple checklists you can hold in your head. The donkey bridges are there to increase your ease of recall.

However, when reading this book, misery is optional. If you hate such gimmicks, feel free to change the words I've used so they no longer create a donkey bridge.

1 Setting the Scene

What is coaching (and mentoring)?

It is customary for the initial chapter of a book to set out the scene, to let the reader know what to expect, to provide some clarification and even definitions of the topic. When I first planned this book, that's what I expected to do. I was assuming that there would emerge, before long, some agreed ways of categorizing and defining various types of **coaching**, including how to differentiate it from **mentoring**.

Time has passed and the coaching and mentoring profession is probably even more confusing than it was. There are many more books available and many more coaching formats. The European Mentoring and Coaching Council (EMCC), of which I was a founder member and then President as it spread across Europe, made a policy decision to refer to **coaching/ mentoring** as a single term. At least, in that way, we felt that people would be prompted to spell out their definitions rather than realizing too late that they had been discussing different things.

Hence, I'm writing this book for you regardless of the type of coaching or mentoring you engage in. I believe that **supervision** and **self-reflection** (both of which I *will* define) are valuable to anyone who engages in an activity that is intended to contribute to the development of another human being. Such activities include approaches other than coaching – consulting and therapy come to mind – but I will concentrate on coaching and I will also invite you to explore the boundaries of coaching and how these influence the processes of reflection and supervision.

I considered including at this point a list of all the labels that are applied to coaching, such as life coaching, sports coaching, executive coaching, and so on. I decided against this in case I left out the label you prefer to use and hence influenced you against reading the rest of the book. Instead I will provide a framework later in this chapter that is intended to help you think about the approach you apply, what distinguishes it from other formats, and what the implications might be for your practice, reflection and supervision.

What is supervision?

This I will define. I think of it as two words – super and vision – as in supervision. To me, it is the process of helping you to step back, metaphorically, from your work so that you can take a meta-perspective, or broader view, of your practice.

This use of the term 'supervision' is of course very different to the way it is customarily used in industry to mean the activities of supervisors or first-line managers when they watch to see that work is undertaken in the way that their organizations (or said supervisors) expect. There may be elements of this managerial function within coaching supervision but the emphasis will be quite different, as will the way it is implemented. People are unlikely to re-view their development needs openly with supervisors who may later in-corporate such information into an annual appraisal and use it to justify a lower salary.

A helpful way to consider the nature of supervision is through three elements described around twenty years ago by Brigid Proctor (1986): nor-mative, formative and restorative. I have renamed restorative as supportive as I think this better captures what is needed for coaches, who tend to encounter less 'distressing' client issues than the counsellors that Brigid was writing for.

For the normative aspects, the supervisor has a responsibility for ensuring that the coach is practising in ways that are competent and ethical. This includes checking that the coach is working within whatever professional, organizational and national rules and laws apply. In other words, it is about ensuring that the coach is behaving as a good coach should and meeting the norms of the profession.

When it comes to formative, the supervisor has a role in the development and growth of the coach and may do this via feedback, direct guidance, role modelling or a variety of other options. The aim is to develop the skills, theoretical knowledge, personal attributes, self-awareness, etc. of the coach so that the coach becomes increasingly competent.

For the supportive element, the supervisor is there to support the coach when the inevitable doubts and insecurities arise, and to challenge and confront (supportively) when the coach's personal issues become evident. This includes providing a safety valve for those times when a coach unwit-tingly seems to pick up the issues that the client has and starts behaving as if these are the coach's own issues. It also includes prompting the coach to see a therapist whenever the coach's own issues are getting in the way.

Harry and Betty

Harry was the supervisor for Betty. Both of them worked within a public sector organization that provided coaching for individuals who were unemployed and hoping to set up their own businesses.

For the normative element, Harry was expected to check that Betty was staying within the boundaries set by the organization, which included providing up-to-date information on grants avail-able, but excluded providing direct assistance with form-filling to claim them. Hence, Harry needed to check regularly that Betty had not only read all grant-change announcements but also that she could explain what such changes meant. Betty was aware that failure to stay up-to-date could mean that Harry insisted on her doing extra study time, and, if that did not rectify the problem, on Betty ceasing to coach until the issue was resolved.

When it came to formative, the organization had a clear policy of developing their staff. Harry was therefore expected to provide feedback, with advice too where appropriate, so that Betty could continually improve her coaching skills. This led to Harry concentrating on a couple of areas where Betty lacked experience.

Finally, for supportive, there were times when Betty's clients became despondent and doubted their abilities to set up successful businesses. Some of this seemed to transfer over to Betty, who began to doubt her own abilities as a coach. Harry was there to listen, empathize and prompt Betty to keep things in perspective, and reassure her that she was doing a good job.

The attention paid to the three elements of normative, formative and supportive will vary according to the type of coaching being practised and the nature of the supervisor/supervisee relationship and context. I am intending at this point in the book to give you just the basic model, which I will develop later. So, in Chapter 2, I will prompt you to consider the balance that is right for you and Chapter 3 will provide some ideas on how you find a suitable supervisor. In Chapter 3, I will also prompt you to think about how these elements may conflict with each other.

Peer supervision, intervision

You can, of course, engage in a process of taking a meta-perspective with a colleague instead of with a formal supervisor. This is often referred to as peer supervision, and sometimes called intervision. You can still use the three elements as a framework.

When it comes to normative, it is not appropriate for someone to accept responsibility for checking that a colleague is doing their job properly. However, with a strong enough relationship, you can certainly draw your colleagues' attention to any potential shortcomings in their professional activity.

On formative, there may be a significant contribution to the supervisee's learning because people often pay far more attention to a colleague's opinions than they do when an authority figure is involved. Comments from those in authority may well be dismissed on the grounds they have no idea what the job is really like. The same comment cannot be dismissed so easily when it comes from a colleague who is actually doing the same job as the supervisee.

Colleagues can be highly supportive *and* challenging. They become involved in similar situations so can empathize from the basis of their own experiences, which also makes it easier for them to spot and challenge inappropriate or inauthentic responses. However, if you engage in peer supervision, you will need to guard against relating too strongly and losing your objectivity.

What is reflective practice?

Reflective practice refers to the same concept as super-vision but without the involvement of a supervisor or colleague. You can reflect as you review your practice across three timeframes – past, present and future. When you reflect on the past, you consider what you have done; how you and the client behaved; what the outcomes were; how you might have acted differently and what that might have led to. Reflecting on the past can be done from memory but may be enhanced considerably through the use of recordings.

When I began training as a transactional analyst, I was introduced to the notion of tape-recording my work and then analysing it afterwards. This was many years ago and taping was an unusual thing to do, even for counsellors and therapists. I quickly saw the benefit of the process even though I had to steel myself to play the tapes to colleagues and my supervisor. I spent a lot of time noticing with horror how many significant aspects of the interaction with the client I'd missed. I was often shocked to realize that I had completed missed something the client had said, or I had failed to pick up at the time on the tone the client used. I also noticed there were parts where I could now, belatedly, identify much better interventions than I had chosen at the time. I persevered and gradually learned to accept these insights and improve my competence for the future instead of beating myself up over my perceived inadequacies.

As you become accustomed to reflecting, it becomes easier to continue the process while with a client and therefore to reflect on the present. Practice builds an ability to run a 'stream of consciousness' reflection in the background of the mind, while still paying attention to the client. You may find it easier to reflect in the present if you choose a simple framework that you can bring to mind without needing to refer to notes. This is what led me to devise the donkey bridges I explained earlier. For instance, using the **C5P5A5** that I will describe in Chapter 5 means that I can easily recall that I want to pay attention to the five aspects starting with a C during the early stages of coaching, then shift to five aspects labelled with a P during the middle stages, and finish off paying attention to five things starting with an A as we reach the end of the session.

The point of reflection is to enhance capability, so time spent reflecting on how to behave in future situations allows you to identify more options and to plan for increased flexibility, with specific clients and more generally. NLP has a technique called future pacing, in which we are invited to go into the future in our imagination. The more vividly we imagine the future scene, the more real it feels. Our brain then records the future scene as if it has already happened. That way, when we reach that specific point in the future, it feels familiar to us and we are therefore more likely to behave in the way we previously chose. This can increase considerably the benefit we get from reflecting.

In addition to the significant learning that comes from reflecting and reviewing, the supervision you receive will be far more effective when you have prepared for it via a process of self-reflection. Prior analysis of your own practice saves supervision time and enables supervisors to operate at a higher level of intensity when they support and challenge you.

> *Michael*
> Michael obtained client agreement to tape-record the sessions. After each session, Michael listened to the tape and noticed that some-times the client spoke so quietly, and Michael interrupted so frequently, that it was as if the client was irrelevant. Michael then selected one occasion on the tape when he seemed to be ignoring the client and analysed what he could hear. Michael realized there was a sequence where the client made a comment and immediately com-mented that 'it's probably nothing'. Michael also then recognized that he felt irritated when he heard that comment, and responded by hurrying the client on to talk about something else.
>
> On listening to more of the tape, Michael could hear more ap-parent 'throwaway' remarks by the client, after most of which Michael talked about something else. Having identified this pattern, Michael was able to plan some other options for the next and future sessions with this client. These included pausing from time to time to encourage the client to say more, confronting occasionally by pointing out that what the client says is 'probably *not* nothing', and questioning occasionally to draw the client's attention to their habitual throwaway remarks. Michael was careful to plan to use confronting and questioning only sometimes, as to do so every time the client made a throwaway remark could well have seemed punitive.
>
> Michael also thought about how interrupting the client had been meeting his own needs and realized that he was working at the

limit of his professional competence with this client so was colluding in overlooking some of the client's issues. Having recognized this meant Michael was able to initiate some support and advice from more experienced colleagues.

Positioning your practice

Before going on to think about your own reflection and supervision needs, take some time to review the format of coaching you apply. What 'type' of coach are you? How is what you do distinguishable from counselling or therapy? What are the boundaries for your work with clients? Figure 1.1 shows a way of thinking about this, based on two key dimensions: whose model of the world, and how much in the here-and-now. Once you've read my explanation of the figure, there are two activities: one set of prompts for positioning your practice and another to help you clarify your reflection and supervision requirements.

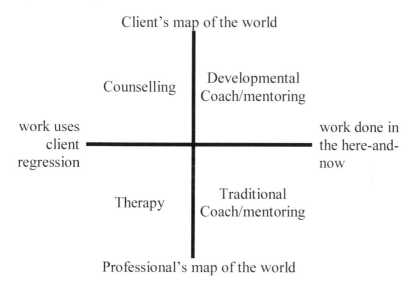

Figure 1.1 Positioning your practice

1 Whose model of the world underpins the work?

Are you working to your own model of the world, with you as the professional, helping the clients to prepare for a future in which they behave in line with the expectations of society (or their organizations)? Are you aiming to be the 'good enough' parent figure or mentor, who interacts with the clients in ways that include role-modelling and providing the kind of experiences the clients may have lacked access to previously?

Or are you intending to be 'non-directive', working within the clients' maps of the world, avoiding any role-modelling or any hint of influence? Are you taking care to identify and set aside your own ideas and opinions? Within an organizational context, is there agreement that the clients may be encouraged to consider options that involve leaving employment – even when they are valued employees?

2 Is the work done in the here-and-now or is the client re-experiencing the past?

Do you aim to have 'here-and-now', reality-based conversations with your clients, during which they are invited to consider various options that may originate from your map of the world or theirs? For instance, a client may propose new career options that you have no experience of, so the two of you then review potential sources of information. Or you may make a suggestion based on your knowledge of a specific vacancy within the company but prompt the client to ensure it is the client's own decision about this rather than simply accepting your proposal.

On the other hand, you may work more deeply with clients, allowing them to regress so that they re-experience events from their past, complete with the original emotions being replayed now and having the same impact they had in the past. We all regress from time to time without realizing it, such as when we sit down in a classroom and feel like we're back in school. If we had a traumatic experience at school, the feelings we replay may be hard to handle. Working in this way requires the ability and resources to provide a secure holding environment so that clients are kept safe while they explore sensitive issues.

Therapists often use involuntary **regression** as a way to enable a client to surface issues from the past that are limiting current functioning. I once heard this described as 'jacking up the house while the client re-arranges the poor positioning of the bricks in the basement'. Note that you can still work with the past without the client regressing. Clients can recall events and talk about them in the here-and-now, so that any strong emotions experienced in the past may be remembered but not felt again with the same intensity.

Four broad approaches

These two dimensions allow us to consider our work in terms of four broad approaches: (1) traditional coaching; (2) developmental coaching; (3) therapy; and (4) counselling. Clearly, there will be times when what we do does not fit neatly into such a box. There may also be counsellors and therapists who do not feel my descriptions of their practice do them justice. However, from the point of view of a coach, this framework will enable you to reflect on how you work and hence clarify your boundaries.

Traditional coaching

I consider traditional coaching to be those ways of working where coaches have some special expertise and/or experience that equips them to act as a role-model or expert adviser. Typically, the organization wishes to have talented individuals developed so they can fulfil defined future roles, or to have someone coached in specific tasks. The mentors or coaches know what competent performance looks like so they decide when coachees or mentees have attained the necessary standard. Note that the recipients are not usually referred to as clients within this approach.

Coaches operating in this traditional format are often highly successful in the areas in which they are coaching. Thus, mentors are frequently senior managers who have demonstrated their ability to operate effectively within the organization. Coaches are likely to be leading practitioners of the skills they teach, albeit that they may have moved on from active participation into coaching newcomers.

Although this approach is run on a here-and-now basis, with the clients being invited to consider what they are learning and review this with the coach, there is still an assumption, often unspoken, that the coach knows best. It is, therefore, the coach's map of the world that counts – this is generally because of the coach's increased awareness of corporate norms and requirements.

Developmental coaching

Developmental coaching is the term I use when the work is based in the here-and-now, with coach and client interacting in logical, discussion-based mode. It differs from traditional coaching in terms of whose model of the world applies. Any additional skill or knowledge possessed by the coach is intentionally suppressed so that the client's map of the world takes precedence.

The coach aims to prompt clients to explore the clients' own world maps so much use is made of questioning and reflecting skills, and of encouraging clients to investigate and explore options. The coach avoids offering opinions or advice, so that responsibility for significant life and career decisions is left firmly with each client.

Organizations that operate developmental coaching schemes are those that recognize that valuable employees are more likely to stay, and work with commitment, if they are treated as gold-collar workers (Kelley 1985) – given opportunities for continual development that are not too closely tied to their current role; invited to consider other options so that they *choose* to stay; provided with evidence that the organization is willing to invest in them.

Such organizations also realize that it is better to lose an employee and recruit a motivated replacement (and free up internal promotion opportunities) than to continue paying the salary of someone who stays in post due to fear of the unknown.

Therapy

There is, of course, any number of formats used by therapists. However, to clarify the differences from coaching, I tend to focus on the way in which therapists utilize regression in order to help clients. Hence, although much therapy will of course take place in the here-and-now, the key to significant therapeutic movement is generally in the way that the therapist responds to a client when that client regresses to childhood or to traumatic events in adulthood.

In addition to creating the holding environment I described above, the therapist acts in the role of 'good enough' parent figure, providing more appropriate responses to clients than were available to them from significant others in the past. This enables clients to work through issues while being supported. This does require, of course, that the therapist/client relationship is sufficiently well established and will continue for as long as needed – something that cannot always be guaranteed for coaching arrangements.

It also needs the therapist to have a map of the world that contains plenty of options for healthy 'parenting' behaviours, and that these cover a range of issues that may arise. It will not help the client if the therapist is shocked by the client's admissions, or cannot provide a supportive reaction. In effect, the therapist needs a map of the world that encompasses much good parenting – in this way, the therapist is able to make good the deficits in the client's experiences of interactions with others.

Counselling

There is probably as much confusion between the terms counselling and therapy as there is about coaching and mentoring. I reiterate that the descriptions I give here are my own and may be challenged. However, in the interests of clarification, I have taken the notion of non-directive forms of counselling for the fourth quadrant. It is similar to therapy in that regression by the client is likely and must be worked with. It differs from therapy in that the client's map of the world is more likely to hold sway.

At the risk of making it sound as if counselling is a 'lite' version of therapy (which it is not), it is generally the case that people seek counselling for issues that they believe to be less serious than those for which they seek therapy. Hence, the regressing tends to be less extensive and there is therefore less need for a re-parenting type of approach. The counsellor can set aside their own world map and work instead with how the clients make meaning.

Activity 1.1 Prompts for positioning your practice

Check out where you 'fit' in the quadrants in Figure 1.1 by considering your responses to the following prompts. In addition to self-reflection, you might review your answers with a peer or supervisor:

- How comfortable are you when people regress and need patience and support?
- How aware are you of your own map of the world?
- How skilled are you at listening and empathizing?
- Do you have specific skills that you could pass on to others?
- How skilled are you at questioning and reflecting?
- Would you enjoy being a role-model?
- Do you prefer to interact with others in rational mode?
- Do you have organizational and/or business experiences to pass on to others?
- How comfortable are you about the maps that others have of the world?

Activity 1.2 Reflection and supervision needs

Having used the above prompts to consider where your practice fits onto Figure 1.1, what are the implications for your reflection and supervision arrangements?

How important are the *normative* aspects?

- Are you able to monitor yourself for competent professional practice (perhaps because you are already a recognized expert in your area of application)?
- What ethical issues might arise in your work – and can you handle these without any involvement of your peers?
- Are you a member of any professional body that requires you to have regular supervision?
- What are the expectations of your clients regarding professional oversight of your work?
- Are there any rules or regulations within your professional context about who would be acceptable as a supervisor?
- Are you a relative beginner who needs a supervisor who can be a role-model and/or provide direct advice and guidance?

How significant are the *formative* aspects?

- Have you finished learning around your area of practice? (This is not meant as a trick question – you may genuinely be 'the' expert in your area and therefore unlikely to learn more content from another.)
- Even though your skills and knowledge may be as advanced as required, how will you benefit from development of your self-awareness and personal attributes?
- Are you a relative beginner who needs a supervisor who can 'teach' you the skills and explain the theories?
- Who do you know (or know of that you could approach) that you believe would stimulate you to personal and professional growth?
- What are the expectations of your clients regarding your commitment to your own development (while you help them to develop themselves)?

How extensive are the *supportive* aspects?

- How likely are client personal issues to arise in your type of coaching practice?
- How likely are your own personal issues to intrude into your practice?
- How much will you need to be able to discuss 'difficult' clients within a safe environment?
- Might you need separate arrangements, such as your own counsellor or therapist, to handle any significant personal issues that affect your professional competence?
- Are you an experienced practitioner – do you need a supervisor who will confront you if you are tempted to stray across the boundary between providing coaching and acting as counsellor/therapist?
- Are you a relative beginner who needs a supervisor who can help you avoid the 'traps' generated by your own and a client's personal issues?

What is transference?

I had intended to include material on **transference** later in the book but realized when I came to write it that it has just as much significance for anyone who is thinking of becoming a coach as it does for their potential supervisors. I am, therefore, including it here so you can check out your responses to Activities 1.1 and 1.2.

In order to explain it, I will also be borrowing from transactional analysis (see various books by Eric Berne or mine entitled *Working it Out at Work – Understanding Attitudes and Building Relationships*) and referring to the concept of **ego states** of **Parent**, **Child** and **Adult**. In particular, I will mention Parent, Child and Controlling Parent, meaning here simply that we behave as if we are parent-like or even as if we are clones of our own parent figures, and child-like or as if we have regressed back into our own childhood. The initial capital letters are used to signify **ego states**, which are ways in which we think, feel and behave, rather than referring to an actual parent or a real child.

Everyday use of English tells us that 'transfer' means something gets shifted across – as in footballers joining new teams. Transference occurs when clients shift across the characteristics of someone else onto the coach. So clients may project their own good or bad points onto you, which will mean that some clients like you a lot because you seem to be just like them and some clients dislike you a lot because they have invested you with their own failings – in this case, the clients probably also manage to repress any awareness of having the faults themselves. This is why it is easier to get on with people once we accept that we are not perfect ourselves. Once we re-cognize that we are still OK even with faults, we no longer have to project those faults onto others and can relate to people as who they really are.

Or it may be the characteristics of someone else that the clients transfer, as when they relate to coaches as if they are parents or caregivers – even to a coach who is younger than the client – or as if the coach is the client's own child, or a niece or a nephew. An interesting variation of this pattern is when a male client relates to a female coach as if she is his mother – potentially reinforced unwittingly by the coach responding as if the client really is a small boy who needs to be scolded. This reaction from the coach is termed **countertransference**. However, what is thought of as countertransference will sometimes be simply the person's own transference.

Professional helpers monitor their reactions for countertransference be-cause this gives them valuable information about how to help their clients. If you recognize feelings of wanting to take care of the client, you can check whether this is a realistic, here-and-now reaction that is also an appropriate thing to do – or whether it is a reaction to helplessness being exhibited by the client. For instance, if a client is clearly unable to deal with being bullied by a local manager, it may be appropriate (and an organizational requirement) for you to report this to senior management. However, a strong urge on your part to intervene with the client's manager over something like management in-terference in a project may be outside the **contract**, part of a **psychological game** of 'Let's you and them fight'; and triggered by a combination of the client's avoidance tactics and your tendencies to act as a rescuer.

When we look more closely at transference, we can identify several for-mats. Michele Novellino and Carlo Moiso (1990), writing of therapy, refer to: the client merging self with the therapist; the client projecting all of the 'good' or all of the 'bad' that the client believes exists within the client onto the therapist; and triadic, where the client projects her or his own Parent ego state, the content of which has been copied from others, onto the therapist.

Petruska Clarkson (1991) wrote about different types of transference: complementary, where the client seeks a symbiotic (meaning co-dependent or sharing one set of ego states) relationship with the therapist; concordant, where the client projects aspects of self onto the therapist so client and therapist seem to be alike; destructive, which is acting out or similar and means therapy cannot proceed; and facilitative transference, where the client chooses a therapist so that the client can still use effective behaviour patterns from the past.

Applying these ideas to coaching, we can categorize on two dimensions: whether we are projecting elements of our self or of someone else (a third party) onto the person we are transacting with and whether we are projecting so that we appear to get on well with the other person or so that we have a problem relating to each other. We can then show four options as in Figure 1.2.

project self

	competitive	concordant	
	we project elements of our own Child or Parent ego state onto the other person and then get into a competitive symbiosis about whose Child or Parent will take precedence	we project elements of our own Child or Parent ego state onto the other person and then believe they are just like us and we are empathizing with each other	
have problem in relating	**conflictual**	**co-dependent**	**appear to get on well together**
	we project elements of 'a third party' onto the other person and then feel we must 'fight' in a Parent-Child or Child-Parent interaction	we project elements of 'a third party' onto the other person and then seek a Parent-Child or Child-Parent relationship	

project someone else

Figure 1.2 Transference formats

Competitive transference

In the following examples, Chris would set up a Parent–Parent competitive pattern, while Vijay would set up a Child–Child competitive pattern. Both create scenarios where there is an apparent rivalry over who gets to exhibit one particular ego state.

Chris was a client who had a tendency to 'take charge' of coaching sessions. Chris would display Controlling Parent behaviour, while at the same time believing that the coach was being overly controlling. Chris would challenge many of the coach's interventions, try to run an agenda and determine time allocations for topics, push forward decisions without giving the coach a chance to intervene, while at the same time complaining that it was the coach who was being overly controlling.

Vijay, on the other hand, would get into a competition with the coach about who was the most needy. Whenever the coach talked about needing a break or asked Vijay to take the lead in a coaching session, Vijay would feel a similar need for a break and would want the coach to take the lead in the next session. In this way, Vijay and the coach would end up competing over who was going to get taken care of while the other one did the work.

Concordant transference

In the following examples, Lauren creates a false Parent–Parent empathy while Peter opts for Child–Child empathy – in both cases the assumptions of being the same mean that the parties avoid certain topics, either because they think their opinions are the same or because they think they know how the other person feels.

Lauren worked as an external coach. When meeting new commissioning clients such as HR directors, Lauren had a tendency to assume that she had the same values about how a healthy organization should operate. This would mean that Lauren made assumptions instead of checking thoroughly to establish the commissioning client's opinions and requirements. With some, the assumptions Lauren made were close enough to reality for it to be virtually unnoticeable. However, every so often, Lauren would have major problems when it transpired later that the commissioning client had very different views. Coaching interventions undertaken by Lauren with individual clients would then turn out to be in conflict with the requirements of the organization.

There are also, of course, commissioning clients who assume the coach shares their opinions, so they commission the work and then rely on trust rather than any accurate monitoring of how the interventions are conducted. Such clients may also conclude that any shortcomings are caused by the individual clients rather than the coach being at fault.

Peter was a coach who would imagine that the client felt the same way, had the same emotional responses and wanted the same things in life, as he did. Peter would therefore feel that a very high level of empathy had been established. This would mean that Peter avoided raising the sort of topics or feedback that he would have found personally upsetting. Because of this, the client was denied opportunities for increased self-awareness and development.

Clients may operate the same kind of transference – they then avoid telling the coach about anything that the coach might find upsetting or embarrassing. Instead, the client censors their own comments and might, for instance, be afraid to use the coach to help them review the pros and cons of leaving the organization because they believe the coach will be upset to lose their client.

Conflictual transference

Lim-Lim has grown up with an overly-controlling caregiver, with whom Lim-Lim had consistently behaved rebelliously (and been punished). Lim-Lim spent several years transferring these controlling characteristics onto managers, and being rebellious towards even the most easy-going of them. This resulted in many Parent–Child interactions in which managers tried unsuccessfully to tell Lim-Lim what to do and Lim-Lim agreed and refused to comply. Lim-Lim began working with a coach who had also grown up with a very controlling caregiver but who had opted to copy that person and therefore unwittingly began to fill the parent role that Lim-Lim seemed to need to rebel against.

Pat had children and had adopted a very Controlling Parent way of behaving towards them. When at work, Pat behaved as if other staff, especially subordinates, were really rebellious children and needed to be treated as such. This led to much conflict – even the fairly easy-going members of staff found themselves feeling resentful and rebellious over the way Pat interacted with them. Pat, of course, saw these reactions as proof of the need to treat people as children.

When someone like Lim-Lim ends up being coached by someone like Pat, they both feel that their views of how to treat people are validated.

Co-dependent transference

Due to circumstances, *Alia* has grown up without nurturing caregivers but had been aware that other children, especially those in films and TV programmes, seemed to have caring parents. Alia was therefore yearning, out of awareness, for such a parent figure. This led Alia to behave in a 'helpless' way, while transferring nurturing tendencies onto almost everyone who was older and/or more senior then herself.

At the same time, *Kim* had grown up in an overly-nurturing environment and had somehow opted to adopt very nurturing characteristics. Having practised with siblings and dolls, Kim was 'programmed' to take care of anyone younger or more junior – so would expect to adopt a Nurturing Parent role to their 'needy' child.

Once Kim became the coach for Alia, they seemed to be locked into a Parent–Child relationship. These ways of behaving led each to believe that the other somehow completed them – in effect they shared one set of ego states.

Note that it is possible to have a healthy dependency of a real child with a real parent. This is because such a relationship reflects reality and does not involve transference – children really do need parenting until they reach a certain age. Couples may also set up functional arrangements that look like transference but are not. For example, one does the gardening and the other cares for the house. No transference is involved as long as both recognize these as *choices* – and know that they are capable of swapping tasks if necessary.

There are several ways in which we can become aware of these processes so they can be eliminated when appropriate. I've referred above to ego states – we can analyse these using questionnaires, feedback from others, role-play or similar activities – anything that helps us recognize how much time we spend in Parent or Child ego states that are reflections of the past rather than being parent or child-like behaviours that we have chosen to use based on current reality.

We can also analyse our interactions, or transactions. The transactional analysis approach uses ego states to check out whether we have com-plementary, crossed or ulterior transactions. A complementary transaction is one where our ego states seem to match, as when we engage in an Adult to Adult problem-solving conversation or match a Parent with a Child response. A crossed transaction might be when we respond to Parent from our own Parent, thereby initiating an argument, or when we respond to a rebellious Child ego state with a problem-solving invitation from Adult. An ulterior transaction is one where what is said on the surface masks some underlying dynamics, such as when we seem to be having a straightforward conversation about some aspect of the client's work while out of our awareness both we and the client are operating on the basis of an unrealistic belief in the power of the coach to miraculously change the life of the client.

Another way of identifying possible transference is to analyse our **stroking**, or recognition, patterns. Eric Berne (1964) coined the term **stroke** to mean a unit of recognition, which is any form of interaction between humans that lets someone know that their existence is recognized by another. So catching someone's eye is a low intensity stroke, speaking to them is more impactful, and hitting or hugging would be a very intense form of stroking. We exchange many strokes with clients in the course of our coaching ses-sions. Because all humans need some level of human contact, we can un-derstand this theoretically as how we give and receive our strokes and can therefore analyse the patterns.

For instance, a coach may take on quite a prominent position in a client's pattern because the experience of receiving unconditional and focused attention may be a fairly rare experience for the client. If clients lacked adequate parenting when they were growing up, they may unwittingly feel as if the coach is now making up the deficit – and come to depend on these extra strokes which they do not seem to get from anyone else. Hence you may come to feel that such clients book sessions they don't really need, or are reluctant to end the coaching arrangement even when the agreed outcomes have been achieved. It can be very tempting to hang on to such clients because they appreciate you so much.

Stroking is of course a two-way process. You may find that the strokes from clients are quite seductive. Having someone act as if you are wonderful because you are helping them can be addictive – you may be reluctant to finish the coaching arrangement at the appropriate time. Claiming feelings of loss and the need to grieve when a client moves on may well be a rationalization of your own loss of the stroking that client was giving you. It is important that you have a healthy stroking pattern in your life generally so you do not become dependent on client strokes and keep a client on just to meet your own needs.

Activity 1.3   Reflecting on transference

- Who does this person remind me of?
- How does interacting with them leave me feeling?
- Are there things I want to say to them that I'm keeping to myself?
- Do I feel drawn to reacting to them in a particular way?
- Do I wish I could behave differently towards them?
- Does the way I'm reacting to them have any similarity to ways I've behaved in the past with other people? Is that significant?
- Do I keep repeating unsatisfactory interactions with this person? Why might that be?
- Do I think this person is being childish? Or bossy? Or helpless? Or argumentative? Or any other annoying way of being?
- Do I get an urge to tell them what to do? Or take care of them? Or argue with them? Or let them take care of me? Or any other inappropriate way of behaving towards them?

The benefits of transference

We may also want to use the transference. It may seem strange to suggest this but therapists do so routinely to enhance their work with clients. A client who thinks the coach is a good parent will be more likely to act on the coach's advice; a client who thinks the coach is 'bad' can be allowed to work through their issues without being punished by the coach. Awareness is the key – once transference and/or countertransference are recognized, the professional uses this knowledge to plan more effective ways of interacting, as outlined in Figure 1.3.

project self

	competitive	concordant	
	Parent – Parent check out the other person's views and paraphrase these; avoid direct disagreement	**Parent/Parent** look for aspects where you have different opinions; emphasize these if necessary	
	Child-Child acknowledge the other person's stated needs; avoid sympathizing and avoid playing 'My problems are bigger than yours'	**Child/Child** look for areas where you experience different feelings; emphasize these if necessary	
have problem in relating	**conflictual**	**co-dependent**	appear to get on well together
	Parent-Child clarify what they want you to do and explore their rationale for this; avoid making excuses or arguing	**Parent-Child** look out for this when someone seems intent on taking care of you; thank them politely (and profusely) and explain you're fine without assistance	
	Child-Parent have a clear rationale when you ask for help; check you do not expect someone else to make your decisions for you	**Child-Parent** watch out for times when you wish someone would take care of you; check whether this is appropriate and, if not, do it yourself	

project someone else

Figure 1.3 Avoiding transference

I can think of many instances where a client or supervisee has behaved as if I were a father-figure. Although I'm female, I have a strong inclination towards acting like a macho male which I do my best to convert into positive controlling behaviour. Being aware of this allows me to act as a role model to let the individual acquire positive ways of being firm when a client has to deal with, for example, an unreasonable colleague.

On other occasions I am perceived as a mother-figure and can then adopt a nurturing style to encourage supervisees or clients to be more confident about their own abilities – such as by expressing confidence in a nervous individual's ability to make a good presentation.

I may also need to avoid transference when I realize that a client or supervisee is making unrealistic assumptions about shared views. In such cases I will explain that I am about to play devil's advocate as a way of prompting the individual to consider other views – or I may of course play devil's advocate without explaining first.

Another example is when I spot the signs of a competitive transference by a client or supervisee. The trap (that I still fall into sometimes) is to end up arguing my point. The antidote is to spend time clarifying the client's or supervisee's ideas and options; this means the individual can't argue with me and I avoid getting into countertransference.

2   Reflection in Action

My explanation of reflective practice in Chapter 1 provides a first simple model to use – set aside time to think about what you've done in the past and what you might do in the future – and take time during coaching sessions to think about the process in the present moment.

In this chapter, I provide some ideas on the practicalities of reflecting. Many of these relate to the past and future timeframes but the very act of reflecting will build up your skills so that you find it easier to do so in the present as well. Later chapters will contain frameworks for the analysis part of reflecting but for now we will concentrate on methods for capturing information and using the available information.

To do this, we can consider the reflection process in a series of stages that continually recycle:

1   Capturing events as they occur.
2   Reviewing specific events.
3   Reviewing a series of events to look for patterns.
4   Planning ahead to incorporate learning points generally.
5   Planning ahead for specific events.
6   Implementing your learning.

Stage 1 Capturing events as they occur

Note-taking

Some coaches make notes during sessions but others prefer not to. The decision on note-taking is yours, preferably in consultation with each client. It will be influenced by personal styles and preferences, as well as by the type of coaching being undertaken. For example, it will be highly relevant during business coaching where the coach provides advice, and contra-indicated while a client is working through sensitive personal issues.

Taking notes will give you a better basis than relying on memory, it will indicate to the client that you are paying careful attention and the notes can then be shown to the client as a check on accuracy. However, taking notes *may* mean that you miss something significant while writing down the previous point, clients may worry about your apparent inability to remember what they say and you may end up quibbling over the accuracy of the notes instead of moving on.

Not taking notes will leave you free to focus your full attention on the client, you will be more likely to pick up on the feelings behind the words, and that will contribute to a relationship that seems more intimate and less businesslike. However, not taking notes may mean that you fail to recall client comments accurately, the client may feel uncomfortable with the intensity of your attention and you may end up quibbling over the accuracy of your recall.

Stream of consciousness

Whether or not you take notes during sessions, it is also useful to get into the habit of writing a 'stream of consciousness' set of notes immediately the session ends. Therapists tend to work with the client for 50 minutes only of the notional therapy hour so they have 10 minutes to do this. As well as capturing as much as possible, it serves as a sort of clearing process – once written down, you can put that session out of your mind and concentrate on the next client.

To use stream of consciousness effectively, it is important that you make no attempt to analyse or evaluate at this stage. Instead, write as much as you can without stopping to edit or think about what any of it means. Include any questions or insights that occur to you as you write, or that you were aware of during the session with the client.

One way to do this is divide a sheet into three columns. In one, you note down whatever you recall of what was said by the client. In the next, you note your own responses, alongside or below each client interaction. Use the third column to note the questions and insights. Work right through the session doing this before you stop to think about what it might mean. Then go back over it, taking your time to reflect on what you've noted. Maybe use a different colour pen to add comments, extra insights, and more questions for you to think about. Finally, go though again and consider what actions you will take, either with this particular client or in general in order to increase your professional competence.

This process is similar to the way well-run assessment centres operate; assessors are trained to write down whatever they notice their candidates doing and saying. Evaluation comes later, when the assessor can comb through the notes to look for evidence of specific competencies. Delaying evaluation in this way avoids the risk of bias setting in and distorting whatever is observed after the first judgement.

Recording

An even better way of generating evidence for subsequent reflection is to record client sessions. Audio recording is enough. Video is possible, of course, but a camera tends to be harder to ignore during the session, raises the issue of whether you point it at coach or client, and is little use for later visual analysis unless you use state-of-the-art equipment. Audio taping also reassures clients because your colleagues and supervisors are less likely to recognize them from voice alone. Video may of course still be useful for training sessions with peers as clients.

When I first began recording my work about 30 years ago, it often required much explanation to clients, who were concerned about how the tapes might be used. Nowadays, that process is much easier as most clients are well aware that any reputable professional will be engaged in continuing professional development. They also understand that coaching consists of human interactions, and that these need to be reviewed and analysed so the coach can become increasingly effective, on behalf of that client as well as generally.

Contracting over the use of tapes is also reasonably common now in organizational settings. Human resource directors and line managers recognize that most coaching relationships need confidentiality and accept that they have no access to the details. The tapes can have the same status as any written notes (and must of course be treated with the same care to ensure no unauthorized access).

I admit to being biased in favour of tapes over notes. This is because 'we don't know what we don't know'. What we write down during and after sessions consists of what we allow ourselves to be aware of. I referred to it earlier as stream of consciousness – and it lacks the unconscious or psychological level, of our interactions. We can't make notes about those aspects that are outside our awareness but if you listen to a tape of yourself you will begin to spot these. You suddenly hear yourself saying something in a particular way, or you notice how you overlooked a client comment, or you recognize a new significance in what was going on. And, once you get beyond the natural tendency to punish yourself for being so unaware at the time, you begin to learn a great deal more about how you function.

Stage 2 Reviewing specific events

Having captured as much information as possible, whether through notes or recordings, the next stage is to initiate a review process. You might do this alone or in a group, with one or more peers, or within a supervisory relationship. You might also use a mix of these formats. Here I will continue to focus on reflection processes that you use alone; there is more on working with peers and supervisors in Chapter 3.

There are of course numerous frameworks that you can use to analyse what you've done. I tend to include mostly models from TA and NLP in this book but you may be familiar with others. The approach or model is less important than the fact that you undertake the process of reflection. In Chapters 4–6, I will outline some specific models that can be used for supervision – any of these can also be used as the basis for self-reflection, as can most of the more general frameworks in Chapters 7–9.

Perceptual positions

For now, though, I think that the NLP notion of **perceptual position**, described by John Grinder and Judith Delozier (1995) is the most relevant for the process of reflection on your own. This apparently simple idea will add significantly to your awareness of the coaching dynamics. It consists of several different 'positions' from which to 'perceive' a situation. You do not actually move – it is as if you observe the situation from different points of view. If you are not familiar with this concept, recall a situation you were in recently with a client or colleague and check it out from each of the positions as they are described below.

In *first position*, you are very much grounded in yourself, being in the moment, feeling and reacting. This should be how you were responding to that client. Maybe you were feeling impatient, or pleased with something the client said, or worried about your own competence to work with this client. You may also have been tuning out the client and thinking about what to have for dinner later, or worrying about the backlog of reports you have to write, or looking forward to an evening at the theatre.

Meta position is concerned with what you were thinking about as you worked with the client. You have 'dissociated' from yourself, detached from your emotional and physical responses, so that you can think about what is happening and analyse the process. Meta here means the opposite of micro – on a computer it would mean that you zoom out rather than in and take in a wider frame. So you may be thinking that another question would be the best option in response to what the client just said, or you have become aware that the client has said something that offends you and you are working to hide this reaction from them, or maybe you have noticed that you got bored and started thinking about tonight's dinner and now need to bring your focus back to the client.

The *second position* is one you may be very familiar with because in this you have metaphorically stepped into the client's shoes, so that you are feeling and thinking as if you are them. This position is the ultimate in empathizing. This is clearly an important perceptual position for a coach to be able to adopt. However, too much of it can become a problem because seeing the world through the client's eyes may mean that the client fails to get the benefit of another point of view from you. Often, the real value of a coach to the client is that of having someone who can challenge their current perspective.

The *third position* is a kind of meta position to both parties, in that you metaphorically step outside the coaching relationship and view it as if you are an impartial observer. Again, this gives you another perspective. What might an unbiased observer notice that you and the client are taking for granted? Which are the areas where you and the client have such similar opinions that you may be failing to challenge the client appropriately? If someone uninvolved were to come along to your session and listen for a while, what feedback would this onlooker be likely to give you, about your own as well as the client's behaviour?

The *fourth position* is harder to explain in words and probably has to be experienced to comprehend. This is the position from which you perceive as if you are the entire relationship – you as coach, your client *and* the interactions between you. This can only be achieved through our imagination, although some would argue that it is a reflection of the real world in which we are all connected at some cellular level, all part of a broader intersecting system.

Finally, although it is not a perceptual position itself, think about the *background* against which the interactions are taking place. This is the context within which the coaching relationship exists, and which is therefore rather like a meta meta perspective, perceiving from right outside. How do your client/coach interactions sit within the overall situation? Are there organizational or cultural elements that have a contextual impact on how the two of you interact?

Activity 2.1 **Perceptual positions**

To reflect on your work, review your notes or listen to your recording while maintaining each perceptual position in turn. You can do this for a complete session or you can select particular interactions and analyse these in depth. If you prefer a more visual approach, try capturing your reactions on each position through a series of drawings. For a more kinaesthetic experience, where you actually feel the sensations at each position, put papers on the floor named for coach and client and actually step onto and around them to represent the various perceptual positions.

Keep notes of what you experience, and of specific learning points, to use in the following stages of reflection and to review with colleagues and a supervisor.

Stage 3 Reviewing to look for patterns

As well as reflecting on specific sessions, it makes sense to review across a series of sessions with the same client and across sessions with your range of clients. In this way, you will be able to identify any repeating themes, or patterns, in how you function.

To make this manageable, you will need to choose some framework for analysis as otherwise there may be too much information for you to process. As for reviewing specific events, you might use the models described in later chapters. For example, you might apply a model of the stages of the relationship, as described in Chapter 4. In that case, you might check the same stage for each of several sessions. Do you have any repeating patterns that occur when you are working to create the relationship with a new client, or any typical stumbling blocks around ending relationships, or do you fall into the trap of advice giving when the client needs to action plan?

Maybe you prefer to use a model that relates to the ongoing process of the coaching such as that in Chapter 5. Do you typically experience concerns about working with clients who have very different backgrounds to you; do you sense that clients are attempting to communicate more than they are saying; or do you feel uneasy about clients who seem to want to be dependent on you?

Or turn to Chapter 6 for the people and contexts parts of the systemic framework, and review whether there are patterns that indicate you are more or less comfortable when the focus is on the coach or the client or the client's contacts, or whether your effectiveness changes according to the type of situation.

Keeping a journal

At this point, let me introduce the idea of keeping a journal or learning log. Your session notes and subsequent reviews may well form the basis for this but the reflections across cases will be even more valuable. Unlike a diary, a development journal will contain far more than your instant reflections on events as they occur. You will use it to capture the themes and patterns you identify across your work.

There are many ways to operate such a journal, which can incorporate colours and symbols to highlight key points, spider maps to show relationships, drawings and even forms of collage for those who are stimulated by more than the written word – plus words are fine too.

At a practical level, you may want sections so you can file individual sessions by client name, with a separate section for your reviews of these sessions (as these are about you rather than the client). Then add a section for your cross-sessional reflections, with perhaps another for your action plans on how you will implement what you are learning. Plus perhaps the final step will be to plan for specific sessions with specific clients, thus closing the loop.

Stage 4 Planning ahead to incorporate learning generally

If you've worked through stages 1 to 3, this fourth stage will be fairly straightforward – you select your learning points and think about how you will use them to develop your professional competence.

You may wish to do some prioritizing at this stage as changing too much too quickly is likely to lead to problems. The **80/20 principle**, based on a pattern identified over a century ago by Pareto (1896/7) and described extremely well more recently by Richard Koch (1997), will help you plan. Put simply, the 80/20, or **Pareto**, rule is that 80/20 per cent applies to anything measured over a large enough group. Hence, 20 per cent of the people in the world own 80 per cent of its resources; 20 per cent of your customers account for 80 per cent of your income; and 20 per cent of your effort leads to 80 per cent of your results.

This latter comment is why the rule matters to us – you can increase your competence significantly through only a small change in your behaviour. The usual difficulty is in identifying *which* 20 per cent will make the difference. However, it is worth making the effort as directing another 20 per cent of effort in the right direction will mean that you get *another* 80 per cent results. That's right – you end up with 160 per cent results based on the 100 per cent you are getting currently. Read Koch if you don't believe this or can't quite understand how it can be possible.

This 160 per cent will of course become your new 100 per cent, generated as before by 20 per cent of your efforts. Hence the importance of continual professional development so that you keep on identifying the next 20 per cent, and the next, and the next...

Activity 2.2   Identifying your 20 per cent

- Review your session notes, journal, etc. to identify which of your interventions appear to be most effective for your clients.
- Do this from the various perceptual positions described earlier in this chapter.
- Seek regular feedback from your clients on what they notice you doing that is particularly helpful (or unhelpful) to them. Incorporate this feedback into your reflection processes.

Distil from the above what you believe to be the 20 per cent that will have the most impact. Go on to the next section for tips on how to implement specific changes into your practice.

Stage 5 Planning for specific events

By planning for specific events, I mean getting ready to work with a specific client in a specific session. Planning vaguely to change or to try out some new techniques will not usually be enough to make it happen. There is much to think about when you are working with a client so avoid adding yet more by having a vague wish list of possible interventions you would like to experiment with. It is also not good practice to use your clients to test out new ways of working on a random basis.

Instead, check first that you have produced your 20 per cent list or something similar. This will mean that you have identified a range of ways in which you intend to develop your competence. Now you can match these to specific clients, choosing interventions that are most likely to help a particular client and to be well received by that client. Make choices that will not be too much of a surprise to the selected client, unless surprise itself would be the best intervention with that client.

At the same time, check that your proposed intervention suits the context, and that you will be able to implement it effectively – if not, get some practice first with a colleague. Remember that coaching skills are like learning to ride a bike – we tend to wobble about a bit at first and may even fall off sometimes before we get our balance sorted out, so it helps to practise in a quiet road to start with.

M&Ms for goal setting

You are probably familiar with one of the variations of SMART for goal setting. A quick look at the internet for this mnemonic shows it may stand for *s*pecific, *m*easurable, *a*ttainable, *r*ealistic and *t*angible, or *s*tated, *m*anageable, *a*ction oriented, *r*esourced and *t*imed, or other variations on similar themes. I prefer **M&Ms**, which I make stand for *m*easurable, *m*anageable and *m*otivational. I re-invented the wheel in this way partly because the three Ms line up with the TA ego states – Parent wants it to be measurable, Adult wants it to be manageable, and Child will only do it if it's motivational.

In addition, I have found that SMART has been used so many times on so many training courses and in so many books that it suffers from over-familiarity so that people are often dismissive of it. For the sweet lovers among you, I also like the fact that you can get M&M sweets instead of Smarties plus a whole range of M&M giveaways such as hats, slippers and sweet dispensers that provide small handful of sweets at a time. This can be a fun way of reinforcing a client's goal setting.

I am writing here about your own goal setting so, unless you feel the need to bribe yourself with sweets, that aspect may apply more to some of your clients. In terms of capitalizing on the learning you get from reflecting on your practice, you can use the M&Ms idea as a set of prompts as you decide how best to implement such learning with specific clients.

First, check if what you propose to do is measurable. Have you stated it in a way that will allow you to measure your success? 'I will ask at least five questions during my next session with David' is measurable whereas 'I will ask more questions' is not. Imagine that a parent figure such as your grandmother will be checking up to see if you did what you were supposed to do, just as she might have done years ago about your school homework. Would you be able to point to a clearly defined outcome and demonstrate that you have achieved it?

Then check if your chosen action is manageable. Is it realistic and within your own control? Asking five questions may not be possible if you have a garrulous client and lack the skills to stop them talking. Planning to get a particular reaction from a client also fails the manageable test as their reactions are up to them. This time, imagine you have a very logical, adult type of person who is interested in the practicalities of your plan – would this person be convinced that what you propose to do is manageable for you?

Finally, ask yourself if your goal is motivational. Are you keen to apply the new behaviour? Does it seem a worthwhile thing to do? Is it likely to have a definite impact on the client that will leave you feeling motivated? Remember the WIIFM (what's in it for me) factor – we put little effort into things that don't enthuse us and hence often fail to have the impact we could. Ask your inner child if it really wants to achieve the goal – if not, then rethink it until you feel enthusiastic about it.

Stage 6 Implementing your learning

Having reflected, reviewed and planned, all that remains is to implement – which brings us back to Stage 1 and capturing the session as it occurs.

You may be aware of the learning styles questionnaire from Peter Honey and Alan Mumford (1986), with its four options of activist, reflector, theorist and pragmatist. The learning cycle was originally described by David Kolb (1984) as that we have a concrete experience, we reflect on it, we pull out the patterns and theories to guide future behaviour, and we decide what pragmatic actions to take next, which will become the next concrete experience. Depending on our learning style preferences, we may start anywhere on this cycle.

Applying this to the contents of this chapter, you started with a concrete experience in that you coached a client. Where possible, you captured this experience as it occurred by taping it. If not, you made notes as soon as possible afterwards in order to capture as much data as possible.

Your experience with the client is the Activist stage of the learning cycle and becomes Stage 1 of your reflection in action process. For Stages 2 and 3, you moved into the Reflector part of the learning cycle. You reviewed specific events and sessions with specific clients. You then reviewed across a number of sessions in order to identify any patterns or repeating themes. For Stages 4 and 5 you moved into the Theorist part of the cycle, pulling out patterns and using theories and models to understand the dynamics so you could plan what to do differently next time. Finally, you have determined some specific actions to take that will implement your learning. As you go ahead with these, you will be completing the Pragmatist part of the learning cycle and coming around again to the next concrete experience.

And so it continues, with you experiencing, reflecting, theorizing and applying for the rest of your professional career.

3   Doing it with Others

In the previous chapter I wrote about reflection as if you might do this alone. Now I invite you to consider how your reflection can be enhanced by working with reflection-colleagues and with a supervisor. When I work with supervisees, I do so on the basis that the responsibility for the process is shared, so that the more supervisees understand about the process, the more they can contribute to its impact. Knowing how the supervision process works is also essential if you want to be able to reflect alongside colleagues.

When this book was being planned, there was some doubt about the relevance of supervision in the title. However, even then the European Mentoring and Coaching Council had included a requirement for regular supervision within the Code of Ethics (although their reference to defining 'suitably qualified' supervisor in the EMCC Standards Document has yet to emerge).

Another factor was the emergence of coaching as a profession. Other professionals, such as psychologists, therapists and social workers, have all had supervision as a requirement for many years. I welcomed the EMCC emphasis on supervision because I have experienced first-hand the benefits of reflecting on my work in the company of a trained supervisor – and, to a lesser extent but still worth doing, with colleagues.

My background has included many years of training in transactional analysis for non-therapy applications. As the use of TA has extended into the organizational and educational fields of application, the potency of supervision became increasingly evident to those of us working in these developmental fields. The requirement, and hence opportunity, to review our work through structured processes of self, peer and supervisor analysis lead to significant increases in self-awareness, ability to analyse 'in the moment', understanding of the process with clients, skills at identifying more options, and all of the extra competence this leads to. Supervision is an extremely effective form of continuous professional development

Discounting

We can understand why supervision, or reflecting with colleagues, is so useful if we are aware of a process known within transactional analysis as '**discounting**'. Rather like discounts in shops, this involves 'taking something off' – instead of the price, it refers to the process whereby people minimize or ignore some aspects of themselves, others or the situation (Mellor and Schiff 1975).

We discount to maintain our sanity. We can only process so much information at a time so we tune out much of the incoming data. For instance, we continue to breathe in and out without conscious attention unless something interferes with our ability to do so – at which time breathing becomes central in our thoughts. Or we cease to notice traffic sounds once we are engaged in a meeting – until sirens sound nearby. At parties, we tune out the background noise to have a one-to-one conversation – until someone mentions our name on the other side of the room.

Unfortunately, this healthy process also runs in ways that are not so helpful to us. Discounting is how we maintain our frame of reference, or map of the world, even when it is out-dated or just plain wrong. Thus, if we believe that someone is always right, we fail to notice any mistakes, whereas if we are sure someone is careless, we overlook any evidence of that person being careful.

The interesting thing about discounting is that we can spot it happening in others but we need others to help us identify our own. In the same way that a coach can recognize what a client appears unable to see, so a supervisor or colleague is often needed if we are to overcome our own discounting.

Discounting occurs at a number of levels of decreasing significance. In therapy, these are generally thought of as treatment levels but I prefer to think of them as **steps to success** – provided someone helps you overcome the discount process, you can climb the steps to a successful outcome. Note that your 'helper' must, however, join you on whatever step you have currently attained. You cannot help someone by functioning from further up the steps, even though that is probably where you are in terms of discounting.

Steps to success

The steps are as shown in Figures 3.1 (a) and (b); the little people are to illustrate how the supervisor needs to come down to the step the coach is on (and sometimes below) in order to 'escort' the coach up the levels.

Level 1: Situation

This is the most serious level of discounting, in which the coach is unaware of the existence of some stimulus within the situation. The coach may fail to notice that the client has smiled or is fidgeting, or may appear to ignore something the client says. When challenged, the coach who is discounting at

(a) The steps

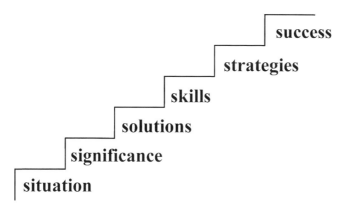

(b) Helping them up the steps

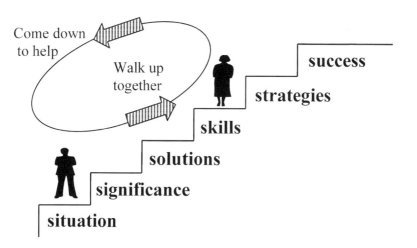

Figure 3.1 Steps to success

this level will seem genuinely puzzled about the aspect that has been overlooked.

Discounting at this level means that no change will occur until the coach is able to bring the situational factors into awareness. Unless the supervisor is extremely intuitive, or good at guessing, this level will only become apparent if the supervision is based on audio or video recordings. Without recordings, the coach will be caught in the trap of not knowing what is being overlooked and may well continue to discount the same stimulus for some time to come.

Level 2: Significance

At this level, the coach notices what is occurring in the situation but discounts its significance. So the coach notices the smile but fails to realize it was inappropriate to the content under discussion, or spots the fidgeting but assumes it was just an uncomfortable chair, or the coach realizes that she or he has spoken over the client but doesn't connect this to the client's wider experiences of being ignored (or the coach's own issues).

This is the level at which a supervisor or colleague can see so easily that someone else has a problem. It is tempting to offer solutions but to do so will result in blank looks (at best) or irritation (at worst). To help, you need to step down to the level of the situation and confirm that the supervisee is aware of the same factors you can see. You can then follow that with questions about what the significance of these factors might be.

Level 3: Solutions

So now the supervisee knows that there are significant elements of the situation – and accepts there is a problem. For some supervisees, this may be enough awareness to move onto problem solving by themselves. However, others will now discount all possible solutions. They may claim that clients often smile inappropriately and there is no way to stop them or that the fidgeting is a necessary release of tension that must be expected, or that coaches are bound to talk over clients sometimes.

As a supervisor, it can be hard at this level not to simply offer solutions. However, the reason discounting occurs is to maintain a frame of reference. Keep in mind, therefore, that the supervisee's psychological equilibrium depends on them continuing to believe that there are no options. There is now the added issue around realizing that if solutions do exist, the supervisee could have solved the problem already – so the supervisee may well be struggling to come to terms with feelings of stupidity or shame for not solving the issue sooner.

Sometimes a supervisee will have a flash of insight at this level and will be able to generate options. Some supervisees may also, albeit ruefully, be able to consider solutions put forward by a supervisor or colleague. The key here will be to ensure the supervisee gives proper consideration to each option and doesn't just accept any proposal for the sake of moving on.

At other times, the supervisee may need more prompting to recognize potential solutions. The concept of **meta programs**, first written about within the NLP literature by Leslie Cameron-Bandler and colleagues (1985) is useful in terms of how to do this. Meta programs are like software for the brain, running in the background and influencing how we behave. There is a meta programme that relates to how we are motivated to act. Research quoted by Shelle Rose Charvet (1997) has shown that around 40 per cent of us respond best when invited to 'go towards' a positive outcome whereas another 40 per cent are motivated by 'moving away from' a negative outcome. The remaining 20 per cent will probably respond to either.

This means that nearly half of us need to be threatened with the stick, while the other half respond best to the promised carrot. To encourage us to recognize the existence of solutions, therefore, we may need to be prompted to consider how much better things can become if we find a way to change, or how much worse if we stay as we are. These positive and negative consequences may also have to be exaggerated until there is enough impact to shift us.

Level 4: Skills

It becomes easier to counter discounting as supervisees move up the steps. By level 4, supervisees will have accepted that there are solutions to be applied. However, they may still seek to maintain a frame of reference that includes the ongoing problem, this time by discounting that they or others have the requisite skills. Someone else might be able to pick up on an inappropriate smile but not them, or their client lacks the skills needed to stop fidgeting anyway, or they doubt they could ever learn to stay silent long enough not to interrupt such a talkative client.

The challenge now for the supervisor is to prompt consideration of what skills are needed and how these can be acquired. The potential trap is of joining a supervisee within a frame of reference that has some people being incapable of learning and changing.

Meta programs can help here too – 'moving away' from supervisees may need to be told they are in the wrong job if they can't grow and develop new skills, while 'moving towards' supervisees can be invited to imagine how many more clients they will help with the new skills they are about to acquire.

Level 5: Strategies

At this level, supervisees have become aware of what is happening and how to resolve it, of what skills will be needed and how to acquire them. If their frames of reference still call for them to maintain the status quo, they will be discounting around strategies for implementing solutions.

Their comments now might be along the lines of being too busy to take on new learning tasks at this time, or lacking a budget for more training or coaching for themselves, or perhaps they have so many new clients at present that they can't find time to plan the necessary behaviour change.

Some fairly detailed questioning may be needed to help them recognize the fallacies behind their 'reasons' for inaction.

Level 6: Success

This final stage is where everything seems to be sorted out but something is still preventing movement. A supervisee may comment vaguely about doing it later. Another may seem highly motivated and enthused but still put off the final implementation.

By now, the supervisor may judge that some overt exploration of the supervisee's map of the world is called for, with particular attention paid to beliefs about success and failure. What are the hidden benefits of taking no action and what are the hidden disadvantages of changing?

Hopefully, most supervisees will work through the higher steps once they have recognized their own discounting around the situation, significance and solutions levels.

Activity 3.1   Dealing with discounting

You may want to work with a colleague for this because it is not easy to spot your own discounting. If based on your own work, you will need to pick an issue where you are already at level 2 – if you have not recognized the significance of whatever is occurring, you can't choose it as an example. Alternatively, ask a colleague to review some of your recordings and identify issues you seem unaware of. Either way, having identified an instance of potential discounting, drop back to level 1 and climb up the steps using the following prompts:

Level 1: Situation

- What is happening?
- Who is saying and doing what?
- What expressions, gestures, body movements are there?

Level 2: Significance

- What might the situational evidence mean?

- If there is an issue or problem, what might it be?
- How is any of this significant?

Level 3: Solutions

- What solutions are available (if you could achieve *anything*)?
- What options might lead to better outcomes?
- What options might lead to worse outcomes?

Level 4: Skills

- What skills do you need to implement various solutions?
- What relevant skills do you have already (including those you've previously used only in different circumstances)?
- How can you acquire any additional skills needed?

Level 5: Strategies

- How will you plan to implement solutions?
- What help or support might you get from others?
- How might others get in your way – and what will you do about that?

Level 6: Success

- What is your rationale for not taking action?
- What are the benefits from not taking action?
- What are you afraid may happen when you take action – and how will you deal with that?

Working with a supervisor

I have included the material on discounting in this chapter with the intention of convincing you that supervision is essential if you are to become aware of the ways in which you limit yourself through your own frame of reference. I hope that you are convinced and ready to consider these options in more detail.

One-to-one or group

The most common format for supervision is one-to-one working between supervisor and supervisee. This may be done privately but can just as easily be conducted in a group setting, with supervisees taking turns. Working privately may mean that a supervisee shares concerns more readily but working in a group has significant advantages. Supervisees can learn much from observing the supervision of others. There are only so many variations of the issues that occur in coaching sessions so chances are high that supervisees will realize that they share the issue currently under supervision, and can work out for themselves what to do next. This leaves them free to bring a different issue when their turn comes with the supervisor – and this may in turn be enlightening for another supervisee.

Another advantage of having supervision in a group is the way that it prompts supervisees to get beyond shame and to realize that mistakes are learning opportunities. It may take a while to pluck up the courage to present aspects of our work where we feel we make mistakes but when we do, we realize that our supervisor and the other supervisees are not judging us. Instead, we are more likely to feel validated by the reactions of others. This is potent learning that enables us to update our frame of reference, and hence empowers us to react to clients in a similar manner.

Yet another benefit of supervision in a group setting is that the 'audience' have the opportunity to monitor their own reactions as the supervision progresses. They can check out whether their own issues are being triggered by what they are observing. If the supervisor runs a short process review after each supervision, there is also the chance to share such reactions and explore how they might be resonating with the supervisee or their client. This can provide valuable additional insights.

The above assumes that the group are an audience of silent observers while one supervisee works directly with the supervisor. This in itself is often a learning experience as some coaches realize that they struggle to stay neutral and silent. If they are giving away their reactions in the supervision group, what impact do they suppose those uncontrolled reactions may be having on their clients? Group supervision can help coaches develop poker-playing skills so they can avoid looking shocked or amused even when clients tell them shocking or inappropriately amusing things.

When a process review is conducted after each supervision slot, it is important that the discussion does not stray back into the piece of supervision. What is to be reflected on is the *process* during the supervision – how supervisor and supervisee interacted, what reactions others experienced, exploration of the supervisor's choices of interventions – but nothing that might re-work the supervision, no direct questions to the supervisee, no attempts to slip in some extra analysis or advice relating to the client.

An alternative way of working with a group is for the group itself to provide the supervision, with the supervisor acting as the back stop. For this, the supervisee in question contracts with the whole group for what she or he wants. This might, for example, be to explore reactions with a particular client, or to consider options for a forthcoming session. The individual members of the group accept responsibility for working within the requested contract, or agree to stay silent if they have nothing to contribute.

Group supervision can be a great way for a supervisee to hear many different perspectives or ideas. It can also be hard work for the supervisor who has to act as a kind of chairperson to ensure that group members keep in mind that the aim is to help the supervisee attain increased awareness and not to push their own opinions. It requires considerable self-discipline for the supervisee to be allowed time to think and respond before the next group member jumps in with their contribution. There is also the risk that the multiple perspectives mean that no one theme is progressed and underlying issues are missed. Plus there is the additional risk of a skilled supervisor stepping in just before the end to do the 'real work', leaving the group to feel inadequate. Group supervision is, therefore, best suited to experienced supervisees who are confident enough to take charge of the process for themselves, and for matters that are relatively straightforward and not linked to deeper personal issues.

Another variant is cascade supervision. For this, one person supervises the supervisee, and that person in turn is supervised on that supervision by someone else, who may in turn be supervised on that supervision by another person, and so on. Again, the 'official' supervisor may be the back stop. This can be an extremely effective way of identifying any parallel process (Searles 1955) that may be in effect.

Parallel process refers to the phenomenon whereby dynamics between people are repeated between others. It often happens that helping professionals react to clients in just the way that said client is reacting to their own contact. For example, 'my spouse is so obstinate' may have the professional thinking 'this client is so obstinate'. It may even have the supervisor thinking 'this supervisee is so obstinate'. Running a cascade increases the likelihood that someone in the sequence will avoid being drawn in to the parallel process.

Group and cascade supervision arrangements are useful for giving supervisees a different, broader perspective on supervision processes. Doing it themselves adds another dimension to their experiences of receiving it.

Working with colleagues

The formats described above for working with a supervisor can of course be utilized without a supervisor. Each group member in turn can contract for what she or he wants, there can be process reviews after each slot, there can be a cascade, and there can be one-to-one slots, privately or within the group setting.

To ensure that peer supervision works well, it is important to take into account normal human difficulties about role switching – it is not easy to be supervisor one minute and supervisee the next. Instead, for one-to-one work, aim to have at least three of you on the group so that person A can supervise person B, person B supervises person C, and person C supervises person A.

R4C4P4 – Ground rules for groups

Consider which of the following might be relevant for your reflection group.

Respect – all opinions are respected and valued, all have equal rights, all will be treated respectfully, we will assume positive intentions for others' behaviours

Responsibility – ground rules can only exist if all involved agree and take personal responsibility. Each person needs to indicate clearly to the rest of the group whether they accept shared responsibility for the ground rules – and for asking for re-negotiation if necessary

Relationship – much development comes from being supported by others, we need to consider how we will support each other, how to establish close and trusting relationships

Results – need to remember purpose, such as to increase self-awareness, develop professional skills, etc. – ground rules need to reflect this emphasis on outcomes and not being simply somewhere to talk about problems

Confidentiality – no-one gossips – what is said in the group room stays in the room (unless the person who said it agrees otherwise)

Commitment – to the group and to ourselves – what we say we will do, we do – or we will explain why we changed our mind

Communication – active listening, one person speaks at a time, plenty of paraphrasing and summarizing to minimize misunderstandings

Challenge – valuable learning comes from feedback – need to give each other honest, constructive criticism (and to balance challenge and support)

Participation – everyone participates – in addition to our own learning, we can help others learn by joining in

Privacy – everyone has the right to pass – to decide not to reveal personal information about themselves, not to give specific feedback to another person

Preparation – all will come prepared to each session, having prepared cases they wish to bring for reflection or supervision in the group

Practicalities – in the real world, things happen that make us late. Time, on the other hand, does not wait. Need to agree how long group will wait for latecomers or whether to start exactly on time anyway – what is routine for people to advise group contact person (and who will do this role?) if they will be late or missing; what will we do about people who miss a session; how many missed sessions before we eject them from the group?

Figure 3.2 Suggested ground rules

Pay particular attention to contracting, so that each supervision slot is set up clearly, and to staying within the boundaries of the contract. Keep in mind that you are supervising and not coaching, so your role is to help the supervisee to take a super-vision of the supervisee's own practice and what that supervisee is doing to help the client rather than how you think the supervisee should have done it. Establish some clear ground rules and agree in advance how you will confront in respectful ways any potential or actual breaches (see Figure 3.2 for some suggested ground rules – **R4C4P4**) Share out the available time and monitor it – don't let people behave as martyrs who give up their time because others have over-run.

Finally, watch out for competitiveness and attempts to fill the vacant leadership slot – groups have a natural tendency to take on the characteristics of their members' families of origin and we need to guard against that. Watch out also for the opposite tendency – of being too nice to each other, getting too cosy and failing to match support with challenge.

Choosing a supervisor

The EMCC Code mentioned at the beginning of this chapter referred to a suitably qualified supervisor. However, coaching is still relatively new as a profession so there are not yet any generally agreed qualifications. At the same time, there are highly qualified supervisors whose previous experience may not include coaching but who might nevertheless be suitable.

Within transactional analysis, for instance, the route to becoming an internationally accredited supervisor involves some five to seven years training plus international examinations to reach analyst status, followed by another five to seven years to qualify as a supervisor. During the latter five to seven years, you are allowed to practise as a provisional supervisor under the overall sponsorship of a fully qualified supervisor (i.e. who has already completed the second lot of five to seven years plus two more international examinations). This qualifying process means that you learn a lot about how to supervise.

There are, of course, non-TA approaches to supervisory training that will be just as thorough, and there are also experienced coaches who will make excellent supervisors even if they lack formal qualifications. You will need to decide what is best for you. You may feel it is important to take into account how much any potential supervisor knows about coaching and what you do, although if you are one of the first in a field it may not be that easy to find such a person.

Another factor to consider is what any potential supervisor knows about supervision. Again, in a new field you may not find a great amount of choice among highly experienced supervisors. You might at least check that any prospective supervisors do at least place a high value on the process of supervision and have arrangements in place to have regular supervision themselves.

Personal characteristics will also be important. Is your potential supervisor a 'good' person who respects and values others? Is the potential supervisor self-aware and growing? Is the potential supervisor professional and ethical?

Activity 3.2 Choosing a supervisor

Consider the following – you may find a yes/no response is sufficient but, if not, try rating each factor from 1 to 10 for importance. You can then check out potential supervisors against your priority ratings, or even compare against the complete profile.

How important is it to you that your supervisor:

- *has experience as a coach?* If you are a beginner coach yourself, this may be essential but if you are fairly experienced you may be able to 'teach' your supervisor what she or he needs to know. Note also that there is a range of coaching typologies – for instance, business coaching may vary considerably from life coaching so that such experience is irrelevant.
- *has experience of the context(s) in which you practise?* Again, as a beginner you may need more of the normative, role-modelling aspects of supervision but if you are experienced, you may prefer a supervisor who can challenge you from a different perspective.
- *has experience of being a supervisor?* If you are new to supervision that may be important, but if you are an experienced supervisee, you may well be able to 'coach' an inexperienced supervisor who had other relevant qualities.
- *has experience of being supervised?* It is harder to imagine why you would want a supervisor who has not been supervised, unless this is your only choice, in which case, you will want to check that such a supervisor's lack of supervision is due to a lack of available supervisors and not an indication of how little value the individual concerned places on the process. Note that professional supervisors continue to have supervision of their supervision.
- *demonstrates understanding and use of theoretical frameworks for her or his own practice and which are relevant to your practice too?* As mentioned in Chapter 1, it is hard to review what we are doing without some constructs and shared language. Consider also whether you will find it better to have a supervisor who knows many theories for a broader range of perspectives or one who uses fewer but achieves greater depth.

- *demonstrates application of theories relating to the process of supervision itself?* It is hard to reflect effectively without some structured models to guide our attention. Chapters 4–6 give some examples but these are not the only options for theoretical frameworks on supervision. It is less important that the supervisee knows the theories of supervision provided the supervisor has a reliable working framework.
- *is respectful of diversity in its many forms and alert to its potential benefits and pitfalls?* If they are, they will respect you and your clients irrespective of race, religion, gender, sexual preferences or any of the other ways in which people are different – and will work actively with difference to maximize the advantages that can come from contrasting perspectives and experiences.
- *is aware of the impact of values, beliefs, assumptions, frames of reference, maps of the world, and so on?* If they are, they will work in ways that take account of your map of the world, and your client's, while also taking care to ensure her or his own map is not biasing the process.
- *has the capacity for self-regulation?* The supervisor will need to foster this in you so it is important that any supervisor is able to monitor her or his own reactions, decide which relate to his or her own issues and which might be useful indicators for you – and also use this awareness skilfully so that you become more self-regulating rather than conforming to the supervisor's uncontrolled reactions.
- *demonstrates a commitment to continuing professional development for self as well as for others?* Most members of professional bodies are nowadays required to maintain CPD logs but it is worth checking out a potential supervisor's attitude to CPD – a chore to keep records or a genuine commitment to seek out opportunities to develop professionally and personally?
- *shows a willingness to abide by an appropriate Code of Ethics and Professional Practice?* Even those who are not members of any professional body can still commit to a 'borrowed' code that fits their circumstances. There are, for instance, non-EMCC members who have chosen to state that they operate to the EMCC Code (although there is of course no route for complaints in this case, so it might be more meaningful for clients if they became members).

Some practical considerations

Having chosen a supervisor or a group of reflection-colleagues, you need to determine how much supervision to have. Various professional bodies set out hours of supervision required per hours of practice but these generally relate to counsellors, therapists, clinical psychologists and the like. The typical client issues for these roles tend to involve deeper psychological processes so it is probable that coaches need a lower ratio.

Hence, if a counsellor is expected to have one hour of supervision for every 6 hours practice, a coach might need only 1 in 12. Of course, this is a guide only and rather like the proverbial piece of string. If you are new to coaching and/or find it stimulates personal issues for you, you will need more supervision. If you are an experienced coach, you may need less supervision, but on the other hand, you may now work with more challenging clients and so you will need more supervision.

There is also a decision to be made about whether you will benefit more from regular supervision or from scheduling supervision to match a varying workload. Should you get supervision weekly or monthly – or have a supervision session after every 12 hours of working with clients – or a mix of both patterns?

And do you need the discipline of scheduling supervision sessions for a minimum number of times (say, quarterly) across the year so you keep the habit even when your workload dips? Or is it more effective to have a series of supervision sessions for a while and then take a break while you consolidate what you have learned?

Your choices of the various scheduling options need to be based on factors such as your preferred learning style and your need to be prompted to move around the learning cycle to maximize your learning, your level of experience as a coach and as a supervisee, and your working patterns, including how central or occasional your coaching practice is. You will probably also need to take into account the nature of your clients and your practice, the expectations of your clients and any organizational **stakeholders**, and, of course, the expectations of the supervisor.

Another factor that will impact on your scheduling of supervision is the timing of the supervision slots. There are some very different opinions about the length of supervision sessions. Coaching sessions often last for an hour or more and I am aware that some supervisors follow this pattern. However, once we get into the sort of in-depth analysis that often involves exploring the coach's own issues, I have found that 20 minutes at a time for an individual supervisee is probably more appropriate. Reflecting and analysing is a challenging and impactful process and my experience has been that after 20 minutes our ability to absorb new learning reduces significantly.

It is possible, of course, to run for longer and pick up several points. However, we need to be careful that this doesn't simply reduce the impact of each aspect addressed. A series of 20-minute slots will mean that the work is far more focused and potent, even if they are run one after the other with some clear punctuations between them such as a couple of minutes break or some re-contracting. Process reviews, when the members of the group reflect on the supervision they have just observed, will help to create natural breaks between slots. It is even better if supervisees can take turns so that their learning has time to settle before they work on the next issue.

I have been writing as if your supervision sessions will be face to face, either with one colleague or supervisor or in a group. It is becoming increasingly common to arrange supervision by teleconference or through a one-to-one phone call. I have supervisees around the world and it is expensive to visit them too often. Without wishing to advertise any particular service, I now use a teleconferencing service and also one that operates via my broadband connection. This latter arrangement allows us unlimited talk time at no additional costs above having the line in the first place. We can also exchange diagrams or texts via our computers, and set up simple cameras at either end so we can see each other. I am not that technologically minded but the set-up procedures were very easy to follow.

One final point on practicalities is cost. I am not going to quote supervision fees in this book because the information will quickly date. However, you can expect that supervisors will charge more than coaches because they will have had to set aside time and money to add supervisory skills to their coaching competencies. My own training as a transactional analyst took about four years whereas my training as a supervisor then took another six years. I also spent two or three years working through NLP practitioner, master practitioner and finally trainer qualifications. I think of this like any other profession – the further you move up the levels, the more it costs you, so the more you expect to charge for your services in order to justify what it has cost you already.

This can be quite a problem for new coaches and many supervisors will be sympathetic and offer financial reductions until a coach has an established client base, especially if the coach trained with the supervisor's organization. I recommend that you ask openly about financial arrangements and be prepared to admit it if you can't afford the fees. Check out also for grants and bursaries that may be available. If you are employed within an organization, make sure that management understand the importance of budgeting for your supervision as well as for your training. If you are in the not-for-profit sector, check out how the question of supervision is dealt with.

Relationships

There are some relationship aspects that also need attention when you are choosing supervisors and reflection-colleagues.

Dual relationships

Dual relationships may generate similar considerations for coaches and clients. A client may be reluctant to 'confess' to weaknesses if the coach is a line manager. Likewise, a supervisee may find it hard to reflect on areas for development if the supervisor has any managerial responsibilities for the supervisee's practice.

It is pointless to insist that these need not be a problem, that supervisees are adults and should be able to manage such a relationship. It is just as unhelpful to say that supervisors should have enough skill to separate their different functions. We are all still human beings and not strictly rational machines.

So it seems that the normative element of supervision may conflict with the formative and supportive aspects. If supervisors are held responsible for the supervisees' work, they will inevitably be tempted to tell the supervisees what to do sometimes rather than letting them learn from their own mistakes.

Where the normative element relates to a shared professional background, it will be easier to offer role-modelling that supervisees can accept or reject. With this relationship, a supervisor will only need to intervene directly to prevent a coach from doing something that will actually be harmful – to the client, the coach or other stakeholder.

However, if the supervisor is also the line manager, then any coach 'errors' may well be counted against the supervisor/manager in her or his own performance appraisal, just as any other shortcomings among the subordinates will be judged as a managerial failure.

It may be that you have no choice and your organization expects your line manager to be your supervisor. In that case, accept the shortcomings of this arrangement and make every effort to find an additional, neutral supervisor, even if you have to sort this out and pay for it yourself.

Another form of dual relationship may arise when a supervisor is also a counsellor or therapist. This may seem beneficial but the nature of the relationship with counsellors and therapists is significantly different to that with a supervisor. You will see this from the material in Chapter 1 on positioning your practice. It is not easy to mix working in the here-and-now with using regression. Once someone has regressed and experienced the nature of relating from that standpoint, it is hard to switch back to here-and-now, two rational adults reflecting together. Even therapists arrange to have a supervisor who is not the same person as their personal therapist. Hence, if you want some therapy on personal issues and find it hard to stay in the here-and-now to work on them, find someone else to undertake the role of therapist for you. That way, you experience two different approaches, with no confusion, and hence both are more potent.

Yet another form of dual relationship that impacts on supervision just as much as it does on coaching is when there are additional social and/or sexual relationships in existence. We know that it is risky to coach our own family and the same difficulties apply to supervision. It is too hard to separate the various strands of the relationship. Confront your supervisees about their discounting and they are likely to take it personally. If you are close enough to supervisees, you will probably have a similar frame of reference in many respects so you won't even notice their discounting because you are discounting in the same way yourself.

One final consideration: however much you aim to work in the here-and-now, the supervision process is likely to involve some element of dependency from time to time. If the supervisor is also a consultant to the supervisee, it will be hard to ensure that any consultancy work (and associated fees) are not being offered to the consultant/supervisor because the customer/supervisee has gone into dependency mode without realizing. Ethically, supervisors need to avoid consulting to supervisees or they need to ensure a third party, such as the supervisee's manager, is asked to check out and confirm any business arrangements.

Symbiosis

I have mentioned dependency and competition. We can understand these dynamics through the process of **symbiosis** as it is applied by transactional analysts. In nature, symbiosis refers to the ways in which two parties are linked for mutual benefit, such as the bird that eats by pecking tics off an animal – without this arrangement the bird starves and the animal dies from tick fever. There is also a healthy symbiosis between a parent and a baby – unless the parent puts aside their own needs to care for the baby, the baby will not survive. So the baby gets looked after and grows and the parent feels fulfilled.

Unfortunately, there are also unhealthy symbioses. Jacqui Schiff, whom I quoted earlier in the piece on discounting, was also responsible for the original TA material on symbiosis. Working with schizophrenics, Jacqui and her adopted son Aaron (Schiff and Schiff 1971) showed how an understanding of the dynamics of symbiosis enabled therapists to plan treatment strategies that brought seriously impaired clients back to normality. This same theory is very useful for coaches and supervisors, albeit that we do of course expect the level of pathology to be considerably reduced.

We can use the concept of ego states, also mentioned earlier, to understand two formats of symbiosis as shown in Figures 3.3 and 3.4. Please remember that initial capitals are customarily used to indicate ego state labels whereas actual parents and children are written in lower case. Also, there are several models of ego states and transactional analysts devote whole conferences to discussing their differing views. I will use a simplified model here because it is enough for our purposes. I will not attempt any detailed definitions as I think it will seem evident from the text that, in the model I am using here, Parent is acting like a parent, Adult like an adult, and Child like a child.

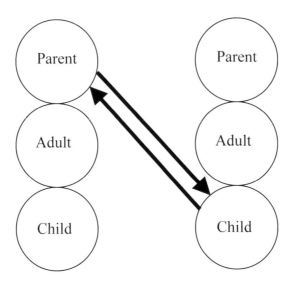

Figure 3.3   Dependent symbiosis

Dependent symbiosis occurs when the two parties seem to 'share' one set of ego state systems. On the basis that a well-functioning human can be thought of as consisting of Parent, Adult and Child, then the healthy arrangement is for the real parent to use Parent (and Adult) to take care of the real child. The real child can therefore concentrate on being in Child ego state until such time as that child has had time to develop her or his own Parent (and Adult) ego state. Over time, parent and child then reach the stage where they have three ego state systems each and can interact in various combinations.

However, things frequently fail to work out as neatly as they might and many people get stuck along the way to adulthood. Hence, the Parent–Child ego state pattern stays too long. Many of us still long, albeit secretly, to be little again and to be taken care of and not to have to deal with the world and its problems. At the same time, some of us grow up expecting to take on the Parent role. So some of us finish up acting helpless like a child and some of us become helpful like a parent.

Hence we finish up in relationships like that in Figure 3.3. One of us parents and the other stays like a child. The more psychologically charged the atmosphere, the more likely there will be such dependent symbiosis. As with any close relationship, the intense nature of supervision presents a powerful pull towards such dependency. Supervisors and supervisees need to look out for any such tendencies if they are to stay in the here-and-now together, using their full sets of ego state systems.

When we are working in a group of supervisees, dependent symbiosis may apply to each of us. Several supervisees may unwittingly feel that the supervisor is their own, personal parent-figure. Apart from the pressure on the supervisor to 'care' for such a large family, this type of situation may lead to sibling rivalry as supervisees endeavour to become the supervisor's favourite.

Competitive symbiosis

Sibling rivalry may also be diagrammed as in Figure 3.4, as a sort of **competitive symbiosis** in which both (or several) parties want to take on either the Parent or the Child role within the relationship. Thus, we may compete to be the Child, and forget that we are grown-up and have an adequate Parent to take care of ourselves, and an Adult with which to problem solve. Discounting will come into play to maintain our frame of reference and we may squabble like the small children we resemble.

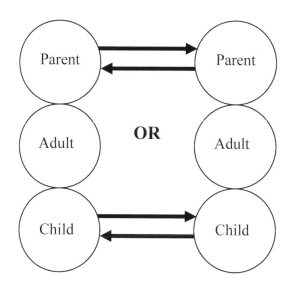

Figure 3.4 Competitive symbiosis

We may also compete to be the Parent. In this case, we expect to define reality. *Our* opinions are what count and others should do as they are told. This will create a dependent symbiosis if those around us are willing to go into Child – but there will be a major competition if two or more of us want the Parent position. Then it will be just like two real parents both insisting they know best.

Avoiding symbiosis

Although a tendency towards symbiosis comes to all of us, it is of course a form of regression. We all unconsciously seek to attain some version of child-like bliss, when parent figures took care of us and we had no need to deal with any of the difficulties of being in the world. So nowadays we discount to maintain frames of reference that allow us to live within such a fantasy. Fortunately, most of us will do that only intermittently, so we have the opportunity to recognize the tendency at other times and plan how to minimize it.

The supervision process is a great way to spend more and more time not being symbiotic. As we become increasingly self-aware through reflection and challenge, we spend more time in the here-and-now. This means we move into being a grown-up, autonomous person, who uses the full set of ego state systems in order to take care of ourselves with our own Parent instead of expecting others to do so – this applies to the controlling, role-setting functions of parenting as well as the nurturing aspects. It also means that we recognize our own wants, needs and feelings within our Child, and are able to separate out those that are relevant reactions to our present circumstances from those, such as fear of ridicule, that are regressions to childhood experiences. In addition, we can then use our Adult ego state to process data, problem solve and make our own decisions. Doing this well requires that we take into account the opinions of our own and others' Parent ego states and the feelings within our own and others' Child ego states – it is not simply a computer-processing sort of decision-making but a fully rounded way of being an autonomous human being.

Supervision also helps us deal with issues such as shame, reluctance to admit mistakes, wanting to be 'super coach', and so on. Once out of symbiosis, we can recognize these inclinations as vestiges of our childhood, when we desperately wanted to please the parent figures. Even the best parents and caregivers have some out-of-date or 'contaminated' material within their frames of reference. This leads to unrealistic expectations, which the small child picks up on intuitively even when nothing is said. The expectations may also be made overt as the parent figure signals clear approval or condemnation.

Few parents or caregivers will knowingly pass on unhelpful expectations to children – they are simply caught up in their own frames of reference. They also believe at the time that they are actually helping the child to become a good member of society. Typically, many of the 'messages' they pass on are outdated or apply only to a small social group or family.

I can give you several examples that illustrate this. Perhaps you were brought up to hide your real feelings and go along with the wishes of others – which may of course make people like having you around, but may also mean they take advantage of you. Or maybe you were encouraged to display and act on your feelings – which may mean you become emotionally intelligent but may also mean you seem to be immature and selfish.

Alternatively, you may have been taught that people with certain characteristics such as skin colour, religion, sexual orientation, etc., are not okay or not to be trusted, or just wrong. On the other hand, maybe you were regarded as the one in the wrong and were criticized for mistakes, or for taking too long, or for getting excited, or staying too calm. Even if your parents did not intend to pass on messages like these, you may have intuitively picked up on their disappointment when you came last in the race, or did something else that disappointed them. Even though your parents did their best to hide their reactions, by not being open about them, you as a child may have concluded that what you did was somehow shameful.

It is fairly easy to imagine how these sorts of messages might impact on us in later years, as we coach and as we get supervision. We may hide our feelings or focus too much on our own feelings and ignore those of the client. We may struggle with prejudice or believe that we are right to be prejudiced. We may be terrified of making, or admitting to, any mistakes, or think we must do our practice and our supervision quickly, or work hard to appear blasé, or become extremely agitated. Or we may convince ourselves we are the worst supervisee in the group, and feel ashamed.

Add to this unwitting 'programming' the fact that some of the messages are created as interpretations by the child and things become even more problematic. Perhaps mother says 'go away' because she has a migraine and the child is too young to know what a migraine is so concludes that mother really feels that the child is unlovable and an unwanted nuisance. Maybe a loved one is rushed to hospital and the small boy believes he caused this to happen by being naughty last week – and thinks the loved one *chose* to go and get away from him. Or the little girl hears the grown-ups talk about how the child is like some other family member – and how that person was no good (or very successful) – and the child may well conclude that she must use the person as a role-model and be just like them.

We can also see how these childhood interpretations may still be running our grown-up lives. We may fantasize that the supervisor or our reflection-colleagues are merely tolerating us and that they wish we would go away. Or we may be scared (probably out-of-awareness but just as powerful an emotion) that we will somehow 'cause' bad luck to those we care about. Or perhaps we take on the characteristics of our supposed role-model – and perhaps compound that by unwittingly slotting others into assigned roles – so that if we are like Uncle Albert or Aunty Mabel, our supervisor may be Grandfather or Grandmother.

There are several techniques that will help us to shift out of the influence of these archaic messages. Reflection generally, and being challenged appropriately by a supervisor or reflection-colleague, obviously help. Working with someone to identify our own discounting and checking directly for positive symbiosis will also be beneficial. Activity 3.3 will also help, as will some of the frameworks in later chapters (especially Chapter 8 on our psychological processes and Chapter 9 on cross-cultural considerations).

Activity 3.3 Avoiding symbiosis

Use the following prompts to identify any tendencies you may have towards symbiosis. Keep in mind that this symbiosis is a natural inclination – don't be too hard on yourself, or your supervisor, when you find the inevitable indications. Instead, use these to prompt enhanced self-awareness and identify options for greater autonomy in the future.

Consider the following in terms of time spent with whoever gives you supervision, including reflection-colleagues.

Parent

- How frequently do I function from a Parent ego state, looking after or attempting to control others?
- How appropriate is this parental behaviour?
- Am I 'parenting' reflection-colleagues instead of challenging them to be autonomous?
- Am I engaging in parent-like competition with my supervisor rather than seeking to gain an alternative perspective on my practice?
- Do I have an adequate internal Parent from which to nurture and challenge myself – and if not, what role-models can I use to develop my own?

Child

- How often do I operate as if from Child, expecting someone else to take care of me, tell me what to do, or even to criticize or punish me?
- Am I competing with reflection-colleagues over who gets most attention, who is most needy, or most fun?
- How else will I behave in future to avoid inappropriate or excessive use of Child ego state?
- How can I meet my genuine childlike needs in other settings so that I will no longer need to sabotage my supervision through being symbiotic?

Here-and-now Adult

- How often do I feel as if I am truly in the here-and-now, interacting with another professional?

- Can I maintain it when it becomes clear during the supervision process that I have been less than competent in an aspect of my practice? When I've made some errors of judgement? When I've really got things wrong with a client?
- What do I need to pay attention to in future to help me stay more fully in the here-and-now?

4 Reflecting on Stages

The previous chapters were provided to establish what reflective practice and supervision involve and to get you interested and hopefully engaged. I now go on to write about the detail of what you should be paying attention to as you undertake your reflection and/or supervision. I begin in this chapter with the most straightforward option – the stages of coaching. I suggest some stages you might use, the key being that you have some form of structure to work to, to ensure you don't overlook anything. Of course, as you become more experienced (as supervisee and supervisor), you will be able to choose how much attention is needed for which stages.

You may well have your own structure for stages when practising as a coach. If so, the following frameworks will serve as examples of how to use this for reflection. If not, then one or other of the following may suit your practice. I suggest that you check out both frameworks below and decide which of them fits best for your practice, assuming you do not have another model already in use. If you do have your own model, then feel free to adapt the activities in this chapter to reflect your own version of the stages of coaching.

The two models I am providing are similar in some respects but one I developed when working on the introduction of mentoring schemes into a number of organizations, while the other arose for coaching schemes. Although I have used the term coaching so far in this book to mean coaching and mentoring, at this point I use the terms separately as a way to differentiate. Key differences were that the mentoring schemes in question involved a broader scope. Mentees were encouraged to consider their entire professional (and personal) lives, including whether they might change careers and employers. The coaching schemes, on the other hand, were designed to assist coaches to acquire greater awareness of organizational norms and the qualities needed to be successful within them.

Note that this is a good example of how the terms can be confusing. In reality, the schemes were quite similar across different organizations. The labels varied partly because of the terminology that had been used previously within an organization, partly because of personal preferences of the person responsible for introducing the scheme, and partly because, over time, it has become fashionable to say coaching instead of mentoring. The labels were also being used in the opposite way to how others often apply them. Hence, I was consulting on mentoring schemes that were developmental rather than traditional, and on coaching schemes that were traditional rather than developmental.

Developmental mentoring

In my 1999 book entitled *Transformational Mentoring*, I proposed the stages listed below – these have been used over the years since in several in-house mentoring schemes:

1   *Alliance* – getting to know each other, agree what we will be doing together.
2   *Assessment* – helping the mentee to assess their current and potential situations, attributes, skills and knowledge.
3   *Analysis* – identifying themes and patterns across time and situations.
4   *Alternatives* – generating options from which the mentee can choose.
5   *Action planning* – prompting the mentee to plan what to do, consider contingencies.
6   *Application* – the mentee implements the action plan, with or without further ongoing support from the mentor.
7   *Auditing* – not really the seventh stage but something that should be continual – this refers to monitoring the relationship as it goes along with a view to constantly enhancing the impact of interactions.

Traditional coaching

In more recent years, I have also been asked to design in-house coaching schemes. For these, I amended the stages to omit analysis because this had generally been done before the decision to undertake coaching. I am writing here of what I think of as traditional coaching, where coachees are selected through some kind of performance assessment and coaches tend to be skills or competence experts.

I 'topped and tailed' the stages with two more components, as shown below. The lines are added to make it clearer that there are five stages with overarching and underpinning components:

> *Supervision* – overarching all stages if the coach is to be supported and challenged to develop their competence.

1   *Starting off* – those activities that take place before coach and coachee come together, such as identification of coaching need and finding an appropriate coach.

2   *Setting up* – establishing a clear contract and effective working relationship.

3   *Stocktaking* – assessing the current situation, skills levels, learning needs, etc.

4   *Strategizing* – working out what needs to be done and doing it, whether this requires 'teaching' from the coach or 'practice' by the coachee.

5   *Saying goodbye* – ending the relationship in a healthy way instead of letting it 'die' or drift on.

Self-awareness – underpinning all stages if the coach is to maximize their effectiveness and minimize the impact of their own issues.

Reflection on stages

There are several ways you can use a framework based on stages to guide your reflection. If you track individual stages as you work through them with a specific client, each reflection session will relate to one stage only, or often to one segment of one stage. You can reflect on how you felt during the stage, what you did, what the client did, and whether you felt any discomfort yourself or sensed that the client was uncomfortable. Discomfort may be a valuable clue that you need to check for any discounting, by yourself or the client.

You can also compare what happens during a specific stage across a number of different clients and see if there are there any similarities that might be reflected on further. Another option is to review how you move from one stage to the next, reflecting on how conscious you are of this process and whether you or the client mark the shift to another stage in some way (a recap or a comment about moving on, perhaps), or do you simply realize afterwards that you somehow moved on without noticing? Alternatively, you might check for any recycling of stages. Was any recycling unavoidable or did you miss something the first time? What impact did any recycling have on the client and is there any pattern to the recycling, such as applying to all stages for one client or the same stage with many clients?

You might also find it enlightening to compare the time spent on each stage. Are there any patterns on time spent that show up across clients? Do you spend significantly longer on some stages? Might you be skipping past some stages? Over a large enough sample, you should find that things average out so any deviations from the norm will be worth exploring with particular attention on what might have prompted you to behave differently in this particular circumstance or with this particular client.

Each of the above formats is likely to generate different insights so applying a mix of them over time is likely to yield benefits. In the following activities, prompts are listed for each stage so you can select an appropriate set.

Activities 4.1–4.7 Reflection on stages: transformational mentoring

---

Activity 4.1   The alliance stage

- How did this relationship start (how did the client and I come into contact with each other)?
- Were other parties involved (e.g. organizational sponsor, referral) and if so, was that simply an introduction or are there any implications?
- What did I do to put the client at ease? To establish a connection?
- What information was shared (before or during the initial sessions) – about me as well as about the client?
- What might the significance be of this information?
- What might not have been said? What might have been said that did not need to be – and what might have prompted such over-sharing?
- What contract has been established? Does it specify procedural, professional and psychological levels?
- How clear are the boundaries to the relationship?
- How are the roles and responsibilities of any other stakeholders incorporated into the contract?
- What are the similarities and differences between me and the client? Are these significant? Have we discussed them, ignored them or pretended they don't exist?
- Whose map of the world has taken precedence?
- How can I tell that the client is ready to move on to the next stage?

Activity 4.2   The assessment stage

- How have we defined the boundaries of what will be assessed?
- What does the client want to cover? Do I need to prompt for areas the client might overlook?
- What are our relative proportions of talking and listening time? Does this need to change?
- What have been the significant questions and prompts I've used to stimulate the client to explore?
- When does the client seem to have closed down? What else might I do to help them open up?
- How have I helped the client to see the overall picture (e.g. by using summaries, or prompting them to sketch spider maps)?
- What have I done to prompt the client to notice and fill in any gaps?

Activity 4.3   The analysis stage

- What have been the significant questions and prompts I've used that have generated insights for the client?
- When do I seem to have 'missed' the client? How else might I help the client to increase self-awareness?
- What models or theories are we using to structure the analysis process? Are these enough?
- How well does the client understand the models being applied? Am I at risk of 'leading' the client through the models?
- Have there been insights that the client has reacted to strongly? Does the client need extra support with these? Or extra challenge?
- What themes and patterns is the client now aware of? Over what timeframe do these apply?
- How do I know when the client is ready to move on to the next stage?

Activity 4.4   The alternatives stage

- How motivated has the client been to generate options?
- How much prompting have I done? Is there any likelihood that I might have been leading the client?
- How broad a range of options has the client considered?
- How have I prompted the client to consider the practicalities of possible options?
- Have I avoided letting the client know whether I approve or disapprove of any options?
- Have we used any problem-solving models? If so, how did this work out? If not, do we need to?
- How have I facilitated the client's process of selecting and discarding options?
- Have I ensured the client thinks about the benefits and pitfalls of each option?
- Have we applied any decision-making models? If so, how did this work out? If not, do we need to?
- Have I challenged the client to double-check any options that seem 'obvious' or that the client thinks are 'too hard'?
- How has the client demonstrated that it is time to move on to the action planning stage?

Activity 4.5   The planning stage

- How have I prompted the client to create an action plan?
- Is the action plan comprehensive enough, without being over-detailed?
- Is the action plan realistic? If not, what can I do to prompt the client to amend it?
- Have we applied any action planning techniques? How did this work out?
- How have I ensured that this is the client's action plan, free of my influence?
- How confident am I that the client intends to carry out the action plan?
- Has the client considered whose help or support might be needed and incorporated this into the plan?
- Has the client thought about who might oppose or undermine this plan and considered how to handle this?
- Which have been my most effective interventions during this stage? Why?
- Which have been my least effective interventions during this stage? Why? What else might I do in the future?
- Will the client still need contact with me during the next stage or will the client implement the action plan without my support?
- How do I know that the client is ready to move on to the application stage?
- How do I feel now that our relationship is coming towards an end? Is there any danger that I am 'hanging on' to the client?

Activity 4.6   The application stage

- Does the client still need contact with me? As often as previously?
- How am I supporting the client during this stage while ensuring the client is not relying on me?
- How am I challenging the client so the client will achieve all that she or he can?
- How am I preparing myself and the client for the end of the relationship?
- What are we doing to celebrate what the client has achieved?
- What – specifically – have I done to encourage autonomy and self-reliance in the client?
- Are there any earlier stages that might need to be re-visited? What can I learn from this?
- How do I feel now that the relationship has run its course? Does this raise any of my own issues?
- What do I need to do to close this relationship and be ready for the next client (or a break)?
- Will I continue in a different relationship with this client? If so, what? Why?

Activity 4.7   Auditing the relationship

This is not really a stage but is a process that can be used throughout the life of the relationship. It can be applied in two ways – by spending a few minutes at the end of each session, jointly reviewing with each client how the session went, and occasionally for a session dedicated to reviewing the relationship to date. This latter application can usefully include a final session as the relationship ends.

You need to create an atmosphere of openness and trust with clients before they are likely to give you honest feedback on your performance. You will also need to react genuinely and positively to whatever they then tell you. The slightest hint of defensiveness or self-justification will mean that clients stop sharing their perceptions or that you end up arguing.

The benefits of auditing are significant. You gain insight into how you come across to each client, which is something you can only speculate about otherwise. It is also a considerable improvement on written evaluations because you can explore what the client really means and discuss alternative ways you might behave in order to be of greater help to the client.

And perhaps most importantly, it signals very powerfully that this is a relationship between equals who share responsibility for the process.

Prompts for reflection and auditing include:

- How frequently do I audit my practice with this client?
- Am I using a mix of short end-of-session audits interspersed with some longer audit sessions? If not, why not?
- What are the most significant pieces of feedback the client has given me? What did I do as a result?
- What are the most challenging pieces of feedback the client has given me? How did I react?

Activities 4.8–4.12 Reflecting on the stages: traditional coaching

Activity 4.8   The starting off stage

- Why did I decide to become a coach? What do I get out of being a coach? (*This is not a trick question – it helps to be aware of our motives.*)
- What type of clients and/or client goals am I likely to be best suited for?
- How do I find my clients or how do they find me?
- How do my clients identify their coaching needs? Is this process adequate or do I need to intervene?

Activity 4.9   The setting up stage

- What have I done to establish rapport with the client?
- What aspects of our working relationship have I discussed with the client?
- How thorough has our contracting been?
- Have I paid attention to what the client may be reluctant to say, or may even be unaware of?
- Have I checked that I am professionally competent in terms of what the client wants to work on?

Activity 4.10   The stocktaking stage

- Have I prompted the client with a variety of frameworks for their stocktaking?
- Have we covered all the aspects that might be relevant?
- How well have I encouraged the client to review their current situation, current competencies, current challenges?
- How well have I prompted the client to identify their learning or developmental needs, skills gaps, etc.?
- How capable has the client been at assessing their own situation and needs?
- How appropriately have I introduced my own assessments of the client's needs (if at all)?

Activity 4.11   The strategizing stage

- What frameworks have I used to help the client work out what she or he needs to do?
- How appropriate has each framework been? Has it assisted the client in achieving the client's outcomes?
- Has there been an appropriate balance between 'feeling or showing' by me and facilitating 'discovery or practice' by the client?
- Who makes the decisions about when the client has achieved the outcomes? Am I a 'judge', does the client decide, or is it by joint agreement?
- What happens if I disagree with the client about the client's progress? How have I handled this?
- Are there alternative sources of evaluation of the client's progress (e.g. line manager, customer)? If so, how have these views been incorporated into our coaching sessions?

Activity 4.12   The saying goodbye stage

- Who decides when the relationship is no longer relevant? How has that decision been made? Against what criteria?
- Are the client and I in agreement that it is time to say goodbye?
- If we decide to continue, are we clear that our future contact will relate to a different client need?
- How do we avoid letting the relationship drift on and on?
- What have we agreed as far as how we will relate if/when we have contact in the future that is unrelated to our coaching relationship?
- What have we done to capture maximum learning from our time together (for both of us)?
- How have we said goodbye in a way that provides healthy closure?

Activities 4.13–4.17 Reflecting on the bigger picture

Activity 4.13   Comparisons between clients

1   Draw up a matrix as shown.
2   Review your reflection notes for a specific stage as undertaken with a number of clients.
3   Use the chart to make notes.
4   Highlight any patterns or themes for further attention.
5   Repeat this for each stage.

Stage	Client A	Client B	Client C	Client D	Client E
What were my key interventions during this stage?					
What did the client achieve during this stage?					
How did the client respond during this stage?					
What concerns did I have?					
What models or theories did we use? How effectively?					
What else did I notice or realize?					

Activity 4.14   Moving from stage to stage

1   Draw up a matrix as shown, using as many rows as you need to insert the stages you work with.
2   Review your reflection notes for a number of clients, paying particular attention to anything that relates to moving on to another stage.
3   Use the chart to make notes so that you can highlight any patterns or themes for further attention.

Stages	Client A	Client B	Client C	Client D	Client E
Moving into					
Moving from Into					
Moving from Into					
Moving from Into					
Moving from Into					

Activity 4.15   Reviewing time spent

1   Draw up a matrix as shown.
2   Chart 1 – sessions or hours: refer to your case notes and/or diary and complete the chart to show how many sessions or hours you spent on each stage with each client.
3   Calculate the average number of sessions or hours spent per stage, by dividing the total by the number of clients.
4   Chart 2 – length of time per stage: produce a second version of the chart and indicate the period of time over which the sessions were run (e.g. three sessions at monthly intervals, so three months assuming next stage started one month afterwards).
5   Calculate the average period of time per stage, by dividing the total by the number of clients.

6   In both charts, look for the stages or clients that are furthest from the average (above or below).

7   Consider why that might be. Are you satisfied that it reflects the needs of the clients? Might it be happening because of your own preferences for particular stages or particular clients?

Stages	Client A	Client B	Client C	Client D	Client E	Total	Average

---

Activity 4.16   Recycling review

1   Draw up a matrix as shown and list the stages in the left-hand column.

2   Refer to your case notes and/or diary to identify any clients where you needed to return to an earlier stage.

3   Note what stage you had reached before you recycled and what led to the need to revisit an earlier stage. Enter a summary of what prompted you to recycle in the appropriate box, i.e. under the client name and opposite the stage you reached.

4   Note against the stage(s) you returned to what then occurred and what the outcome was, i.e. under the client name and against the earlier stage.

5   Add arrows to reinforce the visual image of movement back through the stages.

6   Review the chart to identify any similarities between clients or stages and consider what you might do differently in future.

Stages	Client A	Client B	Client C	Client D	Client E	Total	Average

Activity 4.17   Discomfort and discounting

Coach discomfort can often be an indicator that discounting is occurring. This may be your own discounting or the client's. When the client seems uncomfortable for no apparent reason it may be a signal that you are also discounting, in that you are not allowing yourself to be aware of whatever the client is keeping out of awareness.

1   Draw up a matrix as shown and list the stages in the left-hand column.
2   Refer to your case notes and/or diary to identify occasions when you or your client experienced discomfort that was not resolved during the session.
3   Make notes about the nature of the discomfort in the relevant boxes in the chart, i.e. under client name and against the relevant stage.
4   Look for patterns in terms of client similarities or stages during which discomfort occurs. You may find the steps to success model in Chapter 3 will help you to work out what is being discounted. The following prompts use that model as a basis:
   (a)   What might you or the client be overlooking within the client situation or the coaching situation?
   (b)   What is the significance of the situation? If there is a problem, what might it be? (Go ahead and speculate, ask a colleague for ideas.)
   (c)   Are you or the client failing to recognize potential solutions? Keep in mind that there are always options, even if they are not liked.
   (d)   Is a lack of skill being interpreted as insurmountable? Were you feeling that you lacked the skills to help the client?
   (e)   Is there a problem about choosing appropriate strategies? Were you not sure what to do next? Does the client need to learn action planning techniques?
   (f)   Is an unconscious fear of success preventing you or the client from moving on? Are either of you running a fantasy about the consequences of failure? Do you need to add a touch of realism about what might really happen?

Stages	Client A	Client B	Client C	Client D	Client E	Total	Average

5   Reflecting on Process

In Chapter 4, I included some prompts to think about how you were interacting with your client, how your own reactions might be influencing outcomes, and how discomfort might indicate discounting. However, the
emphasis in that chapter was on the *stages* that you and the client worked
through.

In this chapter, I provide an alternative structure which is based on the
process of your work. By process, I mean the dynamics that occur between a
coach and a client or a supervisee and a supervisor. This chapter is therefore a
fairly lengthy one because I think that reflection on process rather than
content makes a major contribution to our self-awareness and hence our
professional competence. In addition to using it to review your practice, the
structure I provide here can be applied to the supervision process itself. This
enables you as supervisee to take a full share of responsibility for the effectiveness of the supervision. Supervisee feedback is also a valuable gift to a
supervisor.

Within the overall framework I suggest below for reflecting on process, I
have added various theories and models that are likely to be useful as you
consider each element. This has resulted in a chapter liberally sprinkled with
theories and with three extensive activities. Although it may now seem that
the chapter is worryingly packed with information to absorb, let me stress
again that the intention is to provide you with ideas and prompts. I am not
expecting you to work your way slavishly through everything in the chapter.
Instead, choose priority areas and keep your reflection workload manageable
– and enjoyable rather than a chore.

C5P5A5

The basic model I will be using for reflecting on process is something I call
C5P5A5. This is a deliberate donkey bridge which, as I explained at the start
of this book, is a technique for making things more memorable. Thus, this
prompts you to recall that there are five aspects starting with the letter C to
pay attention to, then another five starting with P, and finally another five
beginning with A. The list is given in Figure 5.1. As I said before, if you hate
gimmicks like this, feel free to change the words so they no longer begin with
the same letter. Before you do that, however, check that you will be able to

recall the various aspects when you are in front of a client and want to reflect on the process while still in the midst of coaching.

Note that although this model suggests aspects of process in an approximately chronological order, I am not proposing that these are stages to be worked through dutifully in sequence. Rather, they are elements to be paid attention to, in three clusters – five aspects to pay attention to as you start a session and a relationship, five that are significant during the middle, and five more that generally come at the end.

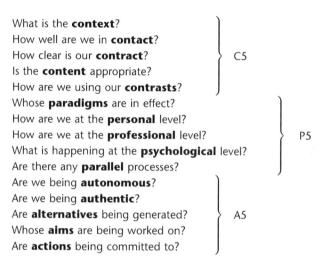

What is the **context**?
How well are we in **contact**?
How clear is our **contract**? } C5
Is the **content** appropriate?
How are we using our **contrasts**?
Whose **paradigms** are in effect?
How are we at the **personal** level?
How are we at the **professional** level? } P5
What is happening at the **psychological** level?
Are there any **parallel** processes?
Are we being **autonomous**?
Are we being **authentic**?
Are **alternatives** being generated? } A5
Whose **aims** are being worked on?
Are **actions** being committed to?

Figure 5.1 C5P5A5

The first cluster consists of *context, contact, contract, content* and *contrasts*. Below are more suggestions to help you reflect on the context within which you and the client (or you and your supervisor) are working, to consider how good the contact is between the two of you, to ensure you have a clearly defined and agreed contract for your work together and that you are working within it, to check that the content of your interactions is within the boundaries of your contract and the context, and that you are extracting maximum benefit from any contrasts or differences between you, whether at the macro level such as race or the micro level such as how you dress (or anywhere in between).

The second cluster prompts you to think about whether you are working to your own *paradigm*, or model of the world, or the client's – or is your supervisor imposing a paradigm instead of working within yours? In addition, how are you now relating to the client (or supervisor) at the *personal, professional* and *psychological* levels? Are there any *parallel* processes, where you might be playing out the same dynamics your client does?

The third cluster, which becomes more significant as the session progresses, contains prompts to check that you and the client or supervisor are both being *autonomous* and not letting someone else decide, and that you are both being *authentic* and not simply pretending to be polite. Is the client (or you as supervisee) considering *alternative* options before making any decisions? Are those decisions based on the client's or supervisee's *aims*? And, finally, is the client or the supervisor committing to clear *actions* arising out of the session?

C5P5A5 can be applied in several ways. You might use it to reflect after any session with a client, to reflect after each stage with a client, or to monitor the process while you work with a client. In the latter case it would of course be used within your own head but not necessarily shared with the client unless perhaps a client that is very advanced and genuinely shares responsibility for the relationship.

It can also be applied as a framework for the auditing suggested in the previously chapter, with you and the client or supervisor using it together. It makes a tool for supervision, this time with the supervisor and supervisee using it together, or inside the head of the supervisor or supervisee who can be running an ongoing reflection or analysis of the process as it occurs.

Finally, it serves as a prompt for reflection after a supervision session as well as before it, and as a way to monitor the process during supervision (in the head of the supervisor or the supervisee)

Some underpinning theories: the C5 cluster

Later in the chapter, I will provide some reflection and supervision activities. First, though, I think it will be helpful to explore some theoretical models that provide insights into various aspects of C5, P5 and A5. Feel free to skip any you are already familiar with – many of the concepts come from transactional analysis or neuro-linguistic programming although the focus on coaching may still be new to you. After each section there will be an activity with prompts for reflection.

Context

Situational anchors
Anchoring is an NLP term for a trigger that has become associated with a specific state of resourcefulness (or often lack of). See a spider and go into a state of fear. Hear the voice of a loved one and go into a state of bliss. Touch a rough surface and feel your teeth go on edge.

Anchors may be behaviours like the examples above but they may also be fixed within the environment. A heated argument during a meeting may create an anchor of the meeting room itself, so that participants are triggered back into argumentative mode whenever they return to the same room. Simply sitting in a room laid out as a classroom is enough to trigger many people into regressing to a childlike state – positive or negative depending on their experiences of school. Baking bread and percolating coffee is a way of triggering prospective house buyers into believing they've found their dream home, if it prompts them into feeling they are back in grandma's home.

The coaching environment is likely to contain **situational anchors** so it is important that these trigger positive reactions. Check out for pitfalls such as using the client's office when this has been the scene of unpleasant incidents, such as being harangued by the boss or pestered by subordinates bringing complaints. Avoid having a seating arrangement that means you are looking down at clients, triggering them into feeling one-down – literally as well as metaphorically. And be careful if you have a secretary or other 'gate-keeper' who may, inadvertently or deliberately, create an atmosphere of you being a 'Very Important Person'.

Watch out also for anchors created during the coaching itself. Clients who have become defensive or distressed during a session may return to the same emotional state as soon as they return to the same chair for the next session. It can be a good idea to make a point of breaking this connection. If possible, changing chairs is a simple method, or you can create a break by making sure that a client has an equally powerful positive reaction while still in the chair. You can also have clients get up and move about and sit down again when they feel more resourceful. It may help in this case to explain what you are doing.

Structure, stimulation and stroking

Our work as coaches, and as supervisors, can be undermined by the context within which the client or supervisee exists. Humans need an appropriate level of structure in their lives. Too little structure and we cannot predict what the likely results of our actions will be. This much ambiguity can be highly stressful. On the other hand, too much structure is also a problem as we feel constrained and unable to make our own decisions.

As well as appropriate structure, we need stimulation. We need an environment that both allows and prompts us to experiment so we can learn and develop. Too little stimulation, especially if combined with too much structure, leads people to play safe and avoid change. Too little stimulation and too little structure may generate a sort of counter-phobic response where we initiate dangerous activities just to feel alive. Too much stimulation may be just as problematic, as we flit from one thing to another, or become hyperactive.

I mentioned in Chapter 1 that I use the term stroking here in the transactional analysis sense of recognition. We all need certain levels of human recognition to stay alive. The experience of Romanian orphans under Ceausescu is a sad reminder that children fail to develop normally without strokes. We also know intuitively that solitary confinement is hard to handle; most of us will settle for negative strokes rather than being ignored. Clients (and supervisees) who lack healthy strokes within their environment may find it hard to choose positive outcomes. They may also come to rely on their coach or supervisor for their stroking needs, making them overly anxious to please, or overly ready to annoy so they get negative strokes.

Structure, stimulation and stroking form a set that needs to be balanced, individually and in combination. Too much structure interferes with stimulation; too much stimulation may lead to negative strokes for lack of results; too little structure leads to negative strokes for transgressing rules that were not clear; too little stimulation may lead to lack of initiative that in turn leads to lack of strokes; and poor stroking patterns may in fact be the vehicle by which inappropriate structure and/or stimulation are conveyed.

It may be necessary to work with clients (or supervisees) on their structure, stimulation and stroking patterns before they can benefit from coaching (or supervision). In extreme circumstances, they may need to consider shifting to a healthier environment. Whether you work on such a scenario with them will of course depend on the nature and boundaries of your relationship with them and any other stakeholder.

Neurological levels

Robert Dilts' (1990) concept of **neurological levels** prompts us to recognize that change must take place at several levels if it is to last. The levels are environment, behaviour, capabilities, beliefs, identity and spiritual, which may better be thought of as community within organizational settings. The model prompts us to consider whether the environment is such that it supports the proposed change, to define the behaviour in terms of what we (or the client or supervisee) need to do differently, and what capabilities, or skills, are required in order to generate the specific behaviours. We then need to check that our beliefs are such that they support and do not undermine the changed behaviour, and that our identity encompasses the requisite beliefs. Finally, we need to be confident that the change will not interfere with our connection with whoever we regard as our community or as our higher power or god.

Behaviour and capability are likely to be well within a coaching or supervision remit. Beliefs and identity will also be taken into account when the importance of attitude is recognized – you can't coach people effectively in customer care while they believe that customers are a nuisance, or if their sense of self precludes any element of caring for others.

Environment and community are the levels that relate to context, and those that may inhibit the client or supervisee from changing even when the other levels have been handled adequately. Consider the organization that initiates an in-house developmental coaching scheme but operates an open-plan policy that means few private places are available for confidential discussions. Or one where no facilities are provided for traditional coaching, so that beginners have to cope with the full job requirements immediately.

Community is the human side of the context. How do clients relate to their organization or team? Is there a supportive environment, with a sense of belonging? Or a hostile environment, or much competitiveness, or a sense of alienation? Clients will struggle to change without a healthy connection to colleagues and management. Similar factors apply for a supervisee – what is the community you are operating within? This can be particularly problematic if you are an independent coach with no regular colleagues, or the only coach within an organization so have no fellow professionals to form a community.

Contact

Calibration
This NLP term **calibration** refers to the process of 'measuring' someone. We calibrate so we can differentiate between different states of being – a common example is that we surmise an embarrassed state when someone blushes and a relaxed state when someone leans back in the chair. I use the word 'surmise' deliberately as we may of course interpret the signals quite wrongly. The blush might actually be part of an allergic reaction and the leaning may be the only way to ease back pain.

To calibrate reliably, we need clusters of clues and we need evidence to confirm what the state really is. Hence, we need to ask questions, listen to responses and observe carefully the signs that the individual is not controlling consciously. These signs will be things such as breathing pattern, tone and tempo of voice, eye (and eyebrow) movements, skin colour, gestures, and so on. We then need to identify what pattern of these signals belongs with which emotion.

Salespeople achieve calibration by asking their prospect questions about previous positive and negative experiences and noting the signals. Then, when the salesperson puts forward a proposal, it is easy to see instantly whether the prospect likes it or not. For a negative, the salesperson can immediately add a comment about maybe it's not quite right and offer an alternative – the salesperson can repeat this 'sliding' process until there is a proposal that the prospect reacts to positively.

Obviously you will not use calibration to sell to your client. However, you can use it to be more aware of client reactions and, as part of that, to ensure you are *not* influencing the client. As you get to know a client, there will be times when you recognize, with a level of confidence, examples such as being uncomfortable around a topic, or getting overly enthusiastic and in danger of rushing into something, or reacting more to please you than on their own decision.

Once you have established some calibration in this way, you will be able to spot when the reactions start occurring again. You can then decide whether you need to change your style of intervention so as to shift the client into a more resourceful state. As you reflect on these occasions, you will be able to build up a checklist of the signals for each.

Another significant factor involving calibration is that many of us calibrate naturally, without realizing we are doing it. We pick up on signals and recognize whether someone is responding positively or negatively. In everyday life this probably keeps us out of trouble. Unfortunately, calibrating without conscious awareness can be a problem when we are working professionally as we may unwittingly adjust our own behaviour to suit.

If we sense that a client is unhappy with our line of questioning, we may move to another topic without realizing what we are doing and the client may miss an opportunity to explore their issues. If we feel that the client is enjoying our interventions, we may do more of the same when something more challenging might have been appropriate.

A similar process may occur during supervision but in that case it may operate in both directions. So the supervisor may calibrate the supervisee, leading to the same problems as with a client – or the supervisee may calibrate the supervisor. It is hard enough to reveal our weaknesses and mistakes to a supervisor, even though we recognize the benefits of doing so, and it is even harder if we are intuitively picking up on the supervisor's negative response.

Representational systems

You may well be familiar with the notion of communication via **visual**, **auditory** and **kinaesthetic** channels, usually referred to within NLP as **VAK**. You may also have some doubts about claims that individuals are predominantly only one of these (although if you think about what someone has to do to convince you that she or he loves you, you may realize that you want to be shown – visual – as in how the person looks at you or gifts you can see, or to be told – auditory – maybe in a specific tone too, or you want to be hugged and held – kinaesthetic).

We are not really confined to one **representational system** but when something really matters to us, we do tend to exhibit certain preferences. Check the chart in Figure 5.2 for clues about what might be going wrong within the various combinations.

Whether representational systems are all-encompassing or not, we can certainly notice how they come into play at times of stress. Our natural tendency then is to shift further into our comfort zone, which includes a concentration on our preferred, or easiest, channels of communication.

'Visual' wants to be shown so needs flowers, gifts	'Auditory' wants to be told, notices tone of voice	'Kinaesthetic' wants to be touched, hugged, kissed
'Auditory' tells them they are loved – 'visual' responds that 'talk is cheap'	'Visual' brings flowers – 'auditory' complains that 'you never tell me you love me'	'Auditory' tells them they are loved – 'kinaesthetic' responds that 'talk is cheap'
'Kinaesthetic' attempts to hug them – 'visual' says 'stop mauling me'	'Kinaesthetic' attempts to hug them – 'auditory' says 'stop mauling me'	'Visual' brings flowers – 'kinaesthetic' complains that 'you never hug me any more'

Figure 5.2 Knowing you are loved – why relationships founder

Hence, at difficult moments most of us will seem to become much more visual, auditory or kinaesthetic.

This applies to both parties. Hence, if we match, there may be little obvious difficulty (apart from missing the opportunity to prompt the client to take a different perspective). However, if we have different preferences, we may end up like a pair who speak different languages.

This may not matter too much once we have a relationship established and indeed, we may deliberately choose different channels then to prompt different perspectives. However, in the early stages a mismatch on communication channels may be much more important, especially as the new client or supervisee is likely to be nervous and therefore less flexible.

Note how the following are all very specific and may therefore create an unnecessary glitch:

- What do you want to talk about? – is easy for auditory
- What do you want to look at? – is easy for visual
- What do you want to deal with? – is easy for kinaesthetic

Instead, use VAK-neutral words if possible, at least until you have identified the client or supervisee preferences, or offer all three options:

- What do you want to achieve?
- What do you want to review?
- What do you want to look at, talk about, and deal with?

Rapport

Rapport may well be the best known, and most misunderstood, of the NLP concepts. Watch people who are getting on well together and you will see that they tend to behave rather like mirror-images, matching each other in four main ways: breathing, body posture, voice tone and tempo, and repetitive movements. So, look around a restaurant and it is fairly easy to spot that those leaning towards each other, or both leaning back, are getting on well while those with one leaning back and one leaning forward seem far less comfortable with each other. Or listen and pick up how close connections seem to have two people talking in similar tones and tempos, such as both enthusiastic or both relaxed, both speaking fast or both slowly, whereas a fast talker and a slow talker have trouble maintaining a conversation, as do an excited and a calm-sounding person.

The key to this apparently obvious concept is that bearing in mind that we naturally match once we have established rapport, we could match from the start so as to achieve rapport more readily. The drawback has been that people have started matching in painfully obvious ways, leaving others bemused or irritated. They have also used the technique clumsily instead of practising elsewhere to build up a level of skill. Finally, some people have been so busy concentrating on observing and copying that it has become obvious that they are not paying any real attention to the other person's comments.

To use this technique well, we need to be subtle. Mimicking their every movement, or changing our accent to theirs, is unnatural and obvious. We need to have practised elsewhere – you don't learn to ride a bicycle on a busy street because you are likely to fall off a few times in the beginning. And it helps if we reach a level of automatic skill, so we can match while still paying close attention to what is being said.

Used skilfully and respectfully, matching will allow us to establish rapport easily and quickly. This will ensure we have a genuine contact with our client or supervisee, making it easier for them to be open about their concerns.

Contract

Levels and the three Rs of contracting

Because it is such a significant concept, I have included a compete chapter on contracting. Thus, Chapter 7 will covers contracting in detail; for now I suggest that you consider at least the three levels: (1) procedural aspects of the contract, such as administration arrangements, documentation, etc.; (2) professional aspects, such as what you are both there to do, what the organization expects, etc.; and (3) psychological aspects, such as all those dynamics that go on under the surface otherwise.

Pre-suppositions

In addition to reviewing those aspects, it can be enlightening to reflect on what **pre-suppositions** may have crept in. Another NLP term, pre-suppositions are those factors which are 'assumed' to be true and which 'must' be true for a sentence to make sense. Thus, 'Will the report be ready for Friday?' implies you have accepted responsibility for producing said report; 'Would you like tea or coffee?' pre-supposes that these are the only options available. Sentences framed with pre-suppositions generally have the effect of 'hypnotizing' the recipient into accepting the implication. So you agree to hurry with the report that you'd not actually agreed to write, or you accept tea or coffee when you really wanted water (or alcohol).

Not such a problem in everyday life, pre-suppositions can seriously jeopardize your contracting. 'Do you want to work on your meeting skills or your decision making?' may lead the recipient to 'forget' that the real reason for coming was to get help with influencing skills. 'When will you talk to your manager?' may push the client into an action the client has not yet fully considered. Even 'How will your partner feel about that?' could prompt the client into feeling the decision has already been made and you may need to pull the client back into considering the pros and cons.

Direction meta program

In Chapter 3, I mentioned meta programs – our software for the brain – and described the one that relates to direction of motivation; *towards* an outcome or *away from* a consequence. This is highly relevant when we are establishing a contract. People who operate an *away from* pattern will focus more on what they want to avoid and may need prompting to sort out what they want instead. Otherwise, they may be vague about potential outcomes and be unable then ever to feel they have reached their goal. Even more problematic is that *away from* motivation tends to run out once they are far enough away from the unwanted consequence. Without a clearly agreed aim, they may well decide the work is finished, only to slide back again until they get close enough to the consequence to become re-motivated to move away from it again.

Reason meta progam

Another meta program that may have particular impact during contracting is *reason*. This involves the dimensions of necessity verses possibility. Some of us aim to change because we feel we *must* or should whereas others change because they *can* or may.

We can pick this program up through speech patterns. 'Necessity' clients or supervisees will talk about how they *must* change, they *should* do better, they *can't* go on as they are. 'Possibility' clients or supervisees will talk about the *opportunity* to change, the *chance* to do better, and that they have come because the option was *available* rather than because they needed to.

Content

Obviously this heading incorporates all we do to reflect on whether the content of our discussions is relevant. Does it fit the contract and the context and is it in keeping with our professional relationship? Whose frame of reference is having most impact on what we talk about? Are we prompting appropriately so that areas of content are not overlooked?

Primary interest meta program

This bit of brain software is about what interests us. It may be that we focus on people, things, activities, places, problems, solutions, ideas, etc. Good coaches prompt their clients to widen their focus of attention – to do this, we need to step beyond our own primary interest.

This program is operating when, for instance, we chat about holidays and one person talks about places visited, another about activities undertaken, another about people met. As the listener, we may pay far more attention to those aspects that match our own preferences, and feel bored by the rest – not a good response for a coach.

Chunk size meta program

This program concerns the level of detail we prefer – large chunk, big picture or small chunk, detailed information. As with primary interest, we can miss each other if we have different preferences.

Clients may need facilitation to move across, so that they create an overview out of disconnected details or flesh out the details of their broad-brush scenarios.

Contrasts

Organizers of coaching schemes often put much effort into the matching process. However, I wonder how useful this really is, when there are so many ways that humans are both alike and different.

We may vary in terms of sex, age, cultural background, ethnic origin, race, religious background, skin colour, sexual orientation, physical attributes, educational experiences, work experiences, social norms, family expectations – and I am sure there are more at this general level. We may also vary in terms of personal styles, behaviour patterns, learning styles, values and beliefs, preferences across a wide range of factors – and again there are more.

Where we are similar, we risk getting too cosy. Where we are different, we risk conflict. We need enough similarity to establish a level of comfort and contact, and enough difference to bring challenge and stimulation to the relationship.

Chapter 9 will expand on differences and how we can operate as effectively as possible cross-culturally. That chapter also provides a summary of stereotypical but nevertheless real differences that have been identified by various researchers and writers.

Reflection using C5: context, contact, contract, content, contrasts

Because C5P5A5 relates to the complete coaching or supervision process, it generates much material for reflection. To make it manageable, I will provide three separate activities: on C5, on P5 and on A5. I do not intend that you should always split your reflection in this way. As you become used to reflecting, you will move naturally from C5 into P5 into A5.

You will also be able to dip in and out as you recognize which elements are most straightforward for you and which provide the most scope for your learning and development. These may change, of course, with different clients, so it is a good idea to re-visit all elements from time to time.

Activity 5.1   Reflection on the C5 cluster: context, contact, contract, content, contrasts

Context

- What is the context for the relationship?
- Who else might have an impact on the client?
- What else might affect how the client behaves?
- What are the boundaries for this relationship?
- What organizational pressures are there?
- What within our immediate environment (the meeting room) might have an impact on the client? On me?
- What patterns of structure, stimulation and stroking exist for the client? How might these affect them?
- Are there any environmental considerations?
- Does the client operate within a supportive or hostile community?

Contact

- How well are we making contact with each other?
- What calibrations have I undertaken? Which 'hidden' reactions can I spot?
- How well have I been matching this client in terms of voice tone and tempo?
- How well have I been matching this client in terms of body posture?
- How well have I been matching in terms of repetitive movements, gestures, and so on?

- Have there been silences during which I've matched body posture and breathing pattern?
- What have I done to facilitate genuine contact with this client at this early stage of our relationship?
- What representational system(s) does this client seem to prefer? Have I been matching their preferences?

Contract

- What other stakeholders need to be taken into account around contracting? Are these involvements overt or implicit? What impact might they have?
- How have we clarified the results or outcomes the client wants? Are these realistic?
- How have we clarified our respective responsibilities? And anyone else's?
- How have we defined our relationship and how we will interact – the personal level of our contract?
- What is the procedural level of the contract for this relationship?
- What is the professional level of the contract for this relationship?
- How do sessional contracts fit within the overall professional contact?
- What might we need to talk about so that it shifts from the psychological level into the professional?
- What pre-suppositions is the client exhibiting? Which need challenging? Have I challenged appropriately? Effectively?
- Is the client motivated to move 'towards gain' or 'away from pain'? What is the impact of this on our contracting?
- Does the client feel she or he *must* be here or is the client responding to the possibilities that coaching stimulates? What is the impact of this on our contracting?

Content

- How does what we talk about match the contract?
- How does what we talk about fit the context?
- Whose frame of reference is determining what we talk about?
- What am I doing to prompt the client to explore areas that seem to have been overlooked?
- What interest areas seem most important to this client (activities, people, problems, etc.)?
- How am I managing any risk of collusion or conflict about what we talk about?
- What chunk size is the client operating? How am I helping the client to consider the big picture and the details?
- What proportion of time is being spent on tangents outside the contract (e.g. pastimes, getting excited about non-related topics, putting the world to rights)?

Contrasts

- How are we different?
- How are we similar?
- How might our differences be helpful to the process?
- How might our differences hinder the process? What interventions might I need around this?
- How might our similarities be helpful to the process?
- How might our similarities hinder the process? What interventions might I need around this?
- What cultural differences might there be between our maps of the world?
- What is my role concerning the client's map of the world (help them develop a different map or respect their current map and leave it alone)?

See Activity 9.1   Fantasies and fears, for more ideas about reflection and/or supervision for this aspect of the process.

More underpinning theories: the P5 cluster

Paradigms

In Chapter 1, I wrote about whose model of the world underpins the work. I invited you to consider whether your professional role meant that you worked to help clients develop within your own model or their own. For instance, you may be operating within an organizationally-based scheme with clear criteria for potential promotion of the client, or you may be a non-directive sounding-board for clients as they determine their own future.

Our paradigms, or models of the world, have a significant impact at many levels. They are often out-of-conscious awareness, making it difficult for us to review them. However, if we approach them through the concept of metaphor we may find it easier to work out what is going on. See Chapter 7 for more ideas about metaphors and how they create boundaries.

Personal

Reflect on how you and the client are relating at a personal level. There are various frameworks you might use – any psychologically-based theory of types will aid self-awareness. Those mentioned elsewhere in this book include working styles in Chapter 8, and Parent, Adult, Child ego states and symbiosis in Chapter 3. Also relevant are two I describe below – MBTI® and Martians/ Venusians.

MBTI®

The **Myers-Briggs Type Inventory**® **(MBTI**®**)** is a popular measure of psychological styles which you may already be familiar with. If not, the following is a brief introduction to the basic elements of it and how it relates to coaching.

MBTI® is a framework for classifying people into 16 types, based on their preferences on four dimensions: their focus of attention; the way they take in information; their decision-making process; and how they relate to the world. It is not essential to complete the MBTI questionnaire – using just the four dimensions provides valuable insights into the way the coach and client are likely to interact.

We all tend to get on best with people of the same type. Being aware of our types means we can guard against conflicts due to type differences – and also watch out for what we might overlook if we both have the same type.

Extraversion/Introversion

Extraversion and **introversion** should not to be confused with everyday uses of similar terms. They refer to where we pay attention – our inner world or our outer world. Extraverts are energized by the outer world, so they like contact with people, go to visit rather than sending a memo, and are likely to network. Introverts, on the other hand, focus on what goes on inside them, prefer to concentrate on concepts and ideas, and will send a memo rather than talk to someone. Note that introverts may seem preoccupied with privacy but are in fact paying attention to their inner world rather than the coach.

Extravert clients will enjoy talking to the coach but may neglect to write up their coaching log. They will readily approach others for help and advice but may dismay an introvert coach with so much networking. They may telephone to talk at times that do not suit the coach – and fail to realize the interruption is unwelcome.

Introvert clients who have agreed to be coached will discuss their thoughts with the coach but may be reluctant to talk to others. They will keep a detailed learning log but may take so many notes during coaching sessions that they lose real communication with the coach. They will attend for planned appointments but may fail to ask for extra support when appropriate.

Extravert coaches may struggle with introvert clients because they expect more contact and discussion than the client wants. There is also a risk that extravert coaches attempt to network for the client instead of encouraging the client to do so themselves.

Introvert coaches may give the impression that they don't want to talk to an extravert client. They may also concentrate too much on the client's thinking processes and not enough on their interactions with others.

Two extraverts together are likely to opt for early action and overlook the need to consider the client's thoughts and feelings. Two introverts together may talk forever about ideas and fail to initiate any action.

Sensing/Intuitive

The **sensing/intuitive** dimension relates to the ways in which we all take in information from the outer world. Even introverts have to exist in the outer world so either of these approaches may be used by extraverts or introverts.

Sensors notice what is actually there. Intuitives 'see' what might be there. Sensors will come to coaching with information about factual matters such as what requirements are written into job advertisements, or the numbers of people employed and their grades. Intuitives will seem to overlook the 'facts' and come to coaching expecting to review possibilities. They notice the potential links between separate situations and the opportunities that might be there.

Sensors will seem grounded in reality but may fail to spot genuine opportunities for development. Intuitives may seize any number of opportunities but may neglect to sort out the practicalities of their ideas before implementing them. If coach and client match, the result may be too much practicality or too much chasing of vague possibilities – and if both are Intuitives, they may actually argue about which imagined possibilities are best. If coach and client are too far apart, they may find it hard to reconcile the different perspectives on the world.

Thinking/Feeling

The **thinking/feeling** dimension concerns the ways in which we make decisions. Thinkers do so based on logic; Feelers take into account their own and others' feelings. Thinkers will be rational, using cause-and-effect sequences to come to a conclusion. Feelers will be values-based, influenced by their own emotions and considering the impact on people of any decisions.

Thinking clients may select a coach who is logically a good choice – perhaps someone who is well situated to provide practical help, or someone who is already known as an experienced and successful coach – or the person who scores most against a checklist of coach qualities. They will then expect to have rational discussions with their coach.

Feeling clients, by contrast, may well choose their coaches based on 'gut-feel'. It will be important for them that their selection feels right. They will also be concerned that the coach holds similar values and beliefs to their own. When making decisions, Feeling clients will want to talk openly about their own emotions and those of the coach. Self-disclosure by the coach will be appreciated and harmony may well be a key concept.

Judging/Perceiving

The **judging/perceiving** scale refers to the way in which we deal with the external world. Judgers like to make decisions; Perceivers prefer to keep their options open. Judgers therefore tend to live in a fairly structured way while Perceivers 'go with the flow'.

Judging clients will want a structured approach to coaching, with a fixed schedule of appointments. They are also likely to appreciate working through distinct stages of coaching, so that they can plan ahead. The same trend will appear in the content of the coaching – they will prefer to deal with issues and make decisions as they go along.

Perceivers, on the other hand, will tend towards more casual arrangements. They may be content to make appointments on a one-off basis, planning the next as they finish a session rather than having several in the diary in advance. They will also be more likely to want to re-arrange appointments because something else has come up – and will accept the same from their coaching partner.

Perceivers have a habit of changing their minds when they obtain more information. They can usually see more than one point of view. Applied to the content of their coaching sessions, this will seem eminently sensible to a coach who is also Perceiving – and infuriatingly indecisive to a Judging coach.

MBTI® is the registered US and UK trademark of Consulting Psychologists Press.

Martians and Venusians

In case you haven't yet read John Gray's (1993) book *Men Are from Mars, Women Are from Venus*, the key idea in it is that men and women are different because they originally came from different planets and are therefore **Martians and Venusians**. Obviously such a view is about a metaphor and is not meant to be politically incorrect – so it's more accurate to say that we have Martians (many of whom, but not all, are men) and Venusians (many of whom, but not all, are women).

So what does this have to do with coaching? Well, we have Martian coaches and Venusian coaches (and, of course, some who are at varying distances between these extremes). It is the extremes that are significant in terms of coaching effectiveness.

Martians are typically fairly direct at problem solving. They go alone into their caves to think through the problem – then, if they cannot resolve it, they ask someone they respect about it, expecting to be given a solution. Venusians, on the other hand, like to gather around the well and talk it over with the other Venusians, with much empathizing – until they solve their own problem or decide they can live with it.

Think of this at home. The Martian complains about work and expects to be offered a solution; the Venusian proceeds to empathize; the Martian complains that the Venusian is making things seem worse. If it's the Venusian who complains about work, the expectation is that the Martian will sympathize – but the Martian simply points out that a good solution would be to leave the job if it is that bad. In either case, the 'complainer' feels totally misunderstood.

We can transfer this into the coaching relationship. A Martian coach/Martian client pair will both expect to identify options based on the previous experience of the coach – and may miss other possibilities. A Venusian coach/Venusian client pair will create a counselling format where the client feels genuinely listened to and valued – and may never get around to any action.

Even more problematic in some ways are the mixed pairs. The Martian coach seems horribly macho to a Venusian client, and believes the client is a wimp. The Venusian coach seems weak and indecisive to a Martian client, and believes their client is abrasive and impatient.

Much traditional coaching operates on the premise that coaches will be Martians. The coach advises the client on what to do to succeed within the organization. Developmental coaching approaches are based on Venusian coaches, who listen and reflect while clients come to their own conclusions about their future development. Coaching schemes fit the organizations they operate within – hierarchies tend towards Martian, and teamworking cultures are more Venusian.

Many organizations that seek culture change unwittingly maintain the old culture through the style of coaching. Coaches are so often senior people, who just happen also so often to be the ones who got to the top through behaving appropriately in the old culture. Selected as coaches, they dutifully pass on the management styles that worked for them in the past.

Professional

As we progress through each coaching session, it makes sense to reflect on the professional aspects of our process with the client. This links back to the nature of our role, the expectations of the client and any additional stakeholders, and the context within which we are functioning.

Consider your responses to the *Positioning your Practice* material in Chapter 1. Are you operating within your chosen professional identity? Are you referring on clients if they need areas of competence that you lack?

Reflect also on how you reconcile the personal and professional aspects of your relationship with each client. Are you a coach who is also friendly, rather than a friend who is playing at being a coach?

Finally, to which codes of ethics and professional practices do you subscribe? Have a look at Chapter 7 if you want to reflect on this in more detail.

Psychological

This is such a significant element of the process that I have included references to it in several parts of this book, including the material on discounting in Chapter 3 – we are simply unaware of much that is going on. Symbiosis, also in Chapter 3, explains why it is so easy for us unwittingly to collude with clients who want to regress and be parented. I will be covering the notion of psychological distances and the impact of these on our contracting in Chapter 7, and will describe psychological games in Chapter 8.

Language patterns

Both NLP and transactional analysis have useful insights about **language patterns**. NLP has the Meta Model (Bandler and Grinder 1975a) and the Milton Model (Bandler and Grinder 1975b). These are based on the recognition that we speak with a surface structure that takes for granted the details at a deeper level. Thus, when we say 'My manager asked for the report', we expect the listener to have the same thoughts as us. However, in terms of the nature of the managerial role, we may report to a very remote senior manager and the listener may imagine a friendly junior manager. When it comes to the way the manager asked, we may have meant demanded but the listener thinks requested. Even the nature of the report may vary, as we are thinking of an extensively researched report that contains recommendations while the listener envisages a short report with key points only.

Obviously, these surface and deep structure discrepancies can lead to significant misunderstandings. They also create hypnotic effects. What we don't say gets assumed; what we do say gets interpreted literally. Thus 'When will the report be ready?' implies that it's your job to write it – you may never question that because you are too focused on answering the part about 'when'. 'I'll try' sends a message about trying rather than doing – having people rephrase this into a clear statement of what they will do will bring about a significant change in their demeanour – or they will comment honestly on what is stopping them.

We can summarize the key patterns under five headings (Hay 1998) as shown in Figure 5.3. My apologies for the NLP terminology in the left hand column if you are not familiar with it – feel free to ignore it and concentrate on the language patterns and the themes.

You can also analyse language patterns in terms of the five **working styles** described in Chapter 8. This helps you to spot when people are moving from their useful working style into their unhelpful **driver** behaviour. The more pronounced the language pattern, the more the person is feeling compelled to behave in a familiar manner even though it is making the situation worse.

Type	Examples	Challenge	Theme
Missing information			
Deletion	I am confused.	What about?	Need to explore **what** is missing, what the speaker is omitting
Comparison	It is better to do it this way.	Better than what?	
Unspecified ref index	They don't listen to me.	Who are they?	
Unspecified verb	Do it now.	What does 'do' mean?	
Nominalization	I broke off the relationship.	What definition of relationship?	
Model of the world			
Modal operator – necessity	We must do it this way.	Who says?	Need to explore **who** thinks this, who the speaker is assuming as an authority
Modal operator – possibility	I can't do it.	Who says?	
Lost performative	This is how we should do it.	Who says?	
Maximization			
Universal quantifier	It always happens.	Always?	Need to explore **when** and **where** it does apply/not apply
General ref index	All dogs are vicious.	All?	
Magic thinking			
Cause–effect	You make me angry.	How do I make you angry?	Need to explore **how** the speaker 'knows' so they realize the lack of true connection
Complex equivalence	You don't bring me flowers any more – you don't love me.	How are these connected?	
Mind reading	You don't love me any more.	How do you know?	
Pre-suppositions			
Pre-suppositions	I want to talk to you before you finish the project.	Query the assumption that you'll finish the project	Need to explore **why** the assumption is made

Figure 5.3 Language patterns

Hurry Ups talk fast, interrupt a lot, finish other people's sentences. **Be Perfects** become increasingly pedantic, and use long sentences packed with lots of details to be sure everything is covered. **Please People** soften everything with comments such as just wondering, maybe, possibly, if you like, and you know – the latter usually said instead of their point so you really don't know for sure what they mean. **Try Hards** sound enthusiastic but go off on tangents as the ideas flow and may not actually finish any of their sentences; they often talk about trying. **Be Strongs** sound calm and monotonous, without emotion, and distance themselves, perhaps referring to themselves as 'one' rather than 'I'.

Parallels

I described parallel process (Searles 1955) briefly in Chapter 3, with an emphasis on how supervisor and supervisee may parallel the dynamics between practitioner and client, which in turn may parallel the interactions between the client and whoever the client is 'bringing' to the session.

When you reflect on your practice, check specifically for any evidence of parallels. If your client is a manager talking about issues with subordinates, do you begin to behave as if you too are a manager with your client as a subordinate? Or do you go in a reverse parallel and begin to feel negative toward the client in a way that is probably just how the subordinates react?

> *Myrtle*
> I can illustrate the P5 factors with the case of Myrtle, an external coach involved in an in-house scheme and working with a 'difficult' client. Myrtle was operating within a paradigm that assumed everyone wants to grow and develop, whereas the client's paradigm was about work being a necessary evil in order to make enough money to maintain a particular lifestyle when not at work. On the personal level, the client was very friendly and regularly invited Myrtle to attend social events where the client was engaged in hobby activities. At the professional level, Myrtle struggled to provide coaching in the way that was being paid for by the organization. Beneath the surface, at the psychological level, Myrtle felt a strong urge to persecute the client for not having more commitment to the organization's development processes; we can imagine that the client resented Myrtle's attempts to force an interest in development. And the parallel process became apparent when Myrtle recognized a strong desire to go and play golf whenever a session was scheduled with this particular client.
>
> The increased awareness from reflection and supervision prompted Myrtle to go back to the organization and rework the

contract to include clear provisions about letting the clients set the agenda, with no compulsion on initiating development activities. She also made a note to suggest to future client organizations that they invite participation instead of treating all employees as if they have identical paradigms. Additionally, Myrtle arranged for some supervision that concentrated specifically on her ability to step outside the familiar paradigm and be more cognisant and accepting of different attitudes to work and development.

Activity 5.2   *Reflection on the P5 cluster: paradigms, personal, professional, psychological, parallels*

Paradigms

- Whose map of the world has been most significant?
- Have I respected the client's map of the world?
- Are there any ways in which I might have imposed my map of the world onto the client?
- What metaphors have arisen? What have they represented?
- If either of us were to be characters in a fairy story, who might we be? What impact has this had on our relationship?
- What do our metaphors embody? How much do they encompass and what might they entail that we don't really want?
- Have I enriched my paradigm by being open to the client's perspective?
- How might I prompt the client to develop a more empowering paradigm?

Personal

- In what ways do our styles differ? What impact has this had on our interactions?
- In what ways are our styles similar? What impact has this had on our interactions?
- How have I adjusted my own style to provide a more challenging experience for the client? To provide a more supportive experience?
- Do I like this client? Do I dislike this client? How am I ensuring that my personal reactions are not undermining my practice?
- Are we relating as grown-ups and avoiding Parent to Child interactions?
- Is the client accepting responsibility for their own decisions? Are we avoiding symbiosis?

Professional

- In what ways is my professional identity evident within this work?
- How well does my professional identity fit the needs of the client?

- Does my professional competence encompass the range of client needs? Do I need to refer the client elsewhere?
- Am I staying within my professional role with this client? If not, why not? What might I need to change?
- Have I taken into account the professional needs of any other stakeholders?
- Is there any conflict between stakeholder needs? Any negative impact on the client?
- What professional practice codes are relevant to this work? Am I applying them?
- Are there any ethical considerations I should pay attention to?

Psychological

- What might we not be saying to each other?
- What might either of us be discounting?
- What might we both be discounting?
- How might we be colluding? To avoid areas of conflict? To avoid strong emotional reactions? To avoid embarrassment?
- How balanced are the psychological distances between us and other stakeholders?
- Is the client regressing? Am I allowing them to regress?
- Are there any indicators of psychological games? Anything repetitive that doesn't feel right?
- What language patterns can I hear? Is the client hypnotizing her or himself to fail? Is the client showing signs of going into driver behaviour?
- What assumptions need to be challenged? How might the deep structure of the language vary? What else might the surface structure mean?
- How does it feel when I put myself into the client's shoes?
- What is my intuition telling me?

Parallels

- Are there any ways in which our interactions might be paralleling interactions that the client has with others?
- Are there any ways in which our interactions might be paralleling interactions that I have with others, including my supervisor?
- Are any parallel processes helpful in that they model effective options for the client?
- Would it help the client to be aware of any parallel processes? Or would it be more appropriate for me to use the parallel process to model what is needed?

More underpinning theories: the A5 cluster

This is the third cluster and relates mainly to the end of the session or relationship. Having reflected on your context, contact, contract, content and contrasts during the early stages, and then considered paradigms, personal, professional, psychological and parallels during the middle stages, it is time to check out how you are drawing things to a conclusion.

Autonomous

Are you, and especially the client, being autonomous? This means being in the here-and-now, aware of what is really going on, taking responsibility for yourself. This should be the case if the P5 cluster checked out but it is worth revisiting this aspect to ensure you maintain a 'clean' process to the end of the session.

In addition to the frameworks described earlier, such as whose paradigm is taking precedence and whether our language patterns are hypnotic, the material on symbiosis in Chapter 3 is also relevant here.

Frame of reference meta program

Often described as internally or externally referenced, this NLP concept alerts us to check whether clients are making their own decisions or expecting us to make decisions for them. This may be quite subtle rather than outright requests to tell the clients what to do. There may be an internal process whereby clients choose options because they *think* it is what we would have chosen, or because they expect us to be pleased. Or clients may reject viable options because they think we won't approve.

Windows on the world

I have renamed the TA concept of **life positions** as **windows on the world**, to make the point that they are in fact distortions in how we perceive the world, rather like the notion of rose-coloured spectacles. The positions consist of the permutations of I, You, and OK, not OK. The here-and-now position, or window through which to view the world, is **I'm OK, You're OK** – humans all have value even though their behaviour may not always be acceptable. Even this can, however, be a problem if it leads to a Pollyanna-ish type of naïve belief in the goodness of everyone. It may be wiser to work on a simple I am, You are, and to check out carefully any tendencies to assume only the best in everyone.

The other windows are more obviously problems. I'm OK, You're not OK leads to arrogance. I'm not OK, You're OK means that clients will believe that they are helpless and you must help them. I'm not OK, You're not OK generates an air of cynicism and even despair.

Awareness of windows on the world can help us ensure that clients are firmly in the here-and-now, making autonomous assessments of their own and others' behaviours and inherent human value.

Neurological levels

I referred to this framework in the earlier section on Context, when the environmental level was the most significant. Now it makes sense to check out the beliefs, identity and community levels. Are clients checking against their own beliefs (perhaps as well as yours but not instead)? How are they in touch with their own sense of identity (and not taking on persona as your client)? What community do they feel connected to (that does not include you)?

Authentic

Having decided that we are both being autonomous, is it worth reflecting specifically on how authentic we are being? How engaged are we with the process and the client, and how engaged is the client? The material on transference in Chapter 1 will be relevant here.

Potency pyramid

Karpman (1968) pointed out that we tend to operate as if we are in a **drama triangle** of **Persecutor**, **Rescuer** or **Victim** when we engage in psychological games. He based this on the ways in which the principal characters perform on the stage.

Someone typically persecutes a hapless victim, and then along comes another person to the rescue, and in rescuing the victim that person persecutes the original persecutor. At which point the victim may well side with their former persecutor and the would-be rescuer falls victim to the two of them. And on it goes – the excitement for the audience is in knowing that such switches will occur but being surprised by when and how.

We can avoid this PRV sequence by opting instead for the **potency pyramid** (Hay 1995) shown in Figure 5.4. This shows that the alternatives to Persecutor, Rescuer and Victim are being appropriately powerful, taking responsibility only for those things that are truly ours, and displaying our own vulnerability. The combination of these three leads to personal potency, hence the name of the diagram.

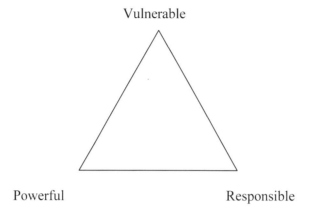

Vulnerable

Powerful   Responsible

Figure 5.4   The potency pyramid

Alternatives

Discounting

A key concept here is to ensure that neither client nor coach is discounting. The material on this in Chapter 3 is relevant, particularly from solutions upwards. Creativity techniques may be useful at the solutions level.

It may also be appropriate to provide information on possibilities if you are satisfied that the client is not discounting but has a genuine gap in their knowledge.

Resourcing

Many of us have skills we use in some situations and fail to apply in others. These 'resources' are available to us but have become locked into specific circumstances. Women returners is a good example – many women will claim to have little organizing ability for an office job yet have been competently running a home, organizing maintenance works, devising school-run rotas, assisting and often managing charity events, and even being the key resource in their partner's business.

We can prompt clients to consider their own range of resources. We can do this by challenging them to identify their current abilities and then force-fitting these into potential new situations. We can also invite clients to 'imagine' they have the skills needed – when imagined vividly enough, the resources begin to exist.

Force field analysis

When a client needs help in deciding which options to pursue, a variation of **force field analysis** as proposed originally by Kurt Lewin (1951) may help. A force field analysis is rather like a balance sheet. You prepare a sheet for each option, with lists of the forces working for that option and against it. An optional extra is to assign a rating to each entry. Totalling the ratings has the effect of giving different weightings to items, so that powerful elements count for more. For example, a decision to change occupation might stimulate the items in the force field shown in Figure 5.5.

FOR	Rating	AGAINST	Rating
enthusiasm for new type of work	10	lack several of the skills	4
will provide a challenge – current job is now too easy	6	would have to attend training programme in own time	6
may stagnate anyway if I stay in current post	10	no good school at new location	7
have attended training course for some of the skills required	4	have just finished decorating present home	7
plenty of support from family	6	estimate a frustrating few months before competent enough to do the job without supervision	8
family prepared to move to new location	5		
organization will pay relocation costs	2		
Total Rating	43	**Total Rating**	32

Figure 5.5 A force field analysis

Aims

This has similarities to the paradigm heading in P5 cluster in that the key question is whose map of the world is taking precedence. Are the aims selected by clients their own or might they have been overly influenced by you?

Ego stating aims

One way to ensure that clients select aims that are truly their own is to prompt them to check against each ego state. Child ego state will be in operation when clients feel they really want the aims or outcomes chosen. Like children who are choosing favoured toys, clients should feel excited by the prospects. Parent ego state may be interfering, just as real parents sometimes prevent real children from having what they want. These real parents may be acting in the child's best interests – but may just as likely be misguided. We all carry 'parent messages' that are left over from childhood and these may interfere with current circumstances even though they are out-dated. Clients may need to be challenged and supported while they re-examine old beliefs that get in the way of living in the current moment. Adult ego state will consider how feasible any aim or outcome is, and will also seek to plan realistic ways of achieving it.

Future pacing

Future pacing, as described by Richard Bandler and John Grinder (1975a), involves imagining yourself in the future and exploring how you feel. This is a useful technique for ensuring that clients are selecting their own aims and not being influenced unknowingly by you. We can prompt clients to do this by having them move along an imaginary timeline while thinking of the aim just selected. As they imagine moving from the present into a point several years in the future, they can check whether things have turned out as expected. If so, have them move another year or so into the future and be aware of looking back to the present, and noticing how things have turned out once the decision was made. If the future is not as the client wishes, have the client come back to the present, change the aims and repeat the future pacing process (as many times as required until the outcome is satisfactory).

Actions

This final element of the A5 cluster will normally signify the end of the session or relationship. Clients will have devised their own action plan and be ready to put them into practice. They may or may not require the coaching to continue during implementation.

M&Ms

I mentioned in Chapter 2 that I prefer M&Ms to SMARTIES. Either model will of course serve the purpose, as would any other frameworks you may prefer to apply. The important thing is that *action* plans are drawn up rather than vague statements of intent.

To apply M&Ms to the coach/client relationship, you are aiming to help the client develop plans that are measurable, manageable and motivational. Measurable so that the end result is clear, so that clients get the satisfaction of knowing they have achieved the objective, and so that the coach also has a way of tracking and celebrating the success of the client. Manageable so that clients can, in fact, achieve the objective, so that they do not set themselves up to fail while trying to do too much, and so that they pick only actions they control themselves and not changes they wish other people would make. Motivational so that they really want to achieve the objective, so that the benefits are obvious, and so that the changes they make will have a positive impact on their future.

Brunhelm was a client who wanted to go and work in France. Figure 5.6 shows how the M & M's were applied to aspects of Brunhelm's action plan.

	Measurable	**Manageable**	**Motivational**
Organize lessons	How frequently? Where? When?	Do I have time to spare?	I like learning this way. I'll meet other students to practise with.
Get books to read	How many? How often? When will I read them?	How much time can I allocate to reading? How much money can I spend on books?	I'll be able to write letters based on what I read.
Plan a touring holiday	When? For how long? Where?	Do I have the time? Can I afford it?	It will really give me the chance to talk French. I'll enjoy it.

Figure 5.6   An M&Ms action plan

Action planning tree

One final framework that may be useful is to take the overall aim, after checking it against M&Ms, and expand it into a detailed 'tree' (see Figure 5.7). This assists the client to turn what may be a hazy, general aim into a number of specific tasks. It is then easy to plan a sensible schedule of activities. Figure 5.7 shows this for Brunhelm.

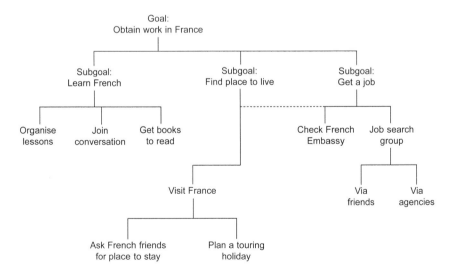

Figure 5.7   Action plan tree

For each item or task, you can prompt clients to consider exactly what needs to be done, who might provide help or support and how might they get that support. Have them also think about what could go wrong and how will they overcome any problems.

Activity 5.3 Reflection on the A5 cluster: autonomy, authentic, alternatives, aims, actions

Autonomy

- Is the client firmly in the here-and-now? Are there any indicators of regression?
- Am I firmly in the here-and-now? Are there any signs that I might be allowing a symbiosis to run?
- How clean are our language patterns? Might I be hypnotizing the client? Might the client be hypnotizing her or himself?
- Whose frame of reference applies? Is the client internally or externally referenced?
- What window on the world is the client running? Is this grounded in reality or contaminated by OK/not OK expectations?
- How does the content fit with the client's own beliefs and their sense of identity?
- How will the client's conclusions fit with the community in which the client operates?

Authentic

- Are there any signs that either of us might be adopting Persecutor, Rescuer or Victim roles?
- How might these be converted into Powerful, Responsible or Vulnerable?
- Might any psychological game be running? If so, what might the outcome be? What can I change to step out of the game dynamics?
- How might I stroke the client so the client has no need of 'gamey' strokes?
- Are there any signs of transference? Is the client clearly in the here-and-now, relating to me as the coach?
- Have I felt drawn to react to the client as if the client is a child or parent? Might that have been countertransference?

Alternatives

- What discounting might have been going on?
- Am I aware of any options the client has overlooked? Have I explored these with the client?
- What have I done to stimulate creativity by the client?
- Have I shared my ideas with the client? Did I do this appropriately?
- How have I helped the client up the steps to success (discounting levels)?

- What resources has the client identified? Does the client need more?
- How might I facilitate the client to find more of the resources the client already has?
- Has the client considered enough alternatives before making decisions?
- How has the client chosen between the various options?

Aims

- Whose aims have been developed? Are they truly those of the client?
- How might I have unwittingly influenced the client? What might I need to prompt the client to reconsider?
- How do the aims identified by the client sit with the client's Child ego state?
- How do the aims identified by the client sit with the client's Parent ego state?
- How do the aims identified by the client sit with the client's Adult ego state?
- How do the client's aims sit with my own Parent, Adult and Child? Has that influenced me or the client in any way? How confident am I that my influence has been only positive and appropriate?
- Have I prompted the client to reflect on the client's own aims, for example, via ego states?
- Did I lead the client through a process of future pacing? Was the client satisfied with the final decision made?

Actions

- How thoroughly has the client checked out her or his motivation?
- How well has the client identified measures of success?
- How carefully has the client reviewed the manageability of the client's plans?
- How thorough is the client's action plan?
- Does the client still need any support from me? Am I sure of that?
- What pitfalls has the client foreseen and planned to overcome?
- Has the client identified enough sources of support? Without relying too much on me?
- Is it time for this relationship to end? How will I handle that ending with the client?
- If the relationship is continuing, how sure am I that continuation is meeting the client's needs and not my own?

6 Reflecting Systemically

In this chapter, I build on the well-established seven-eyed framework of Peter Hawkins and Robin Shohet (2000). I urge you to read the original work if you have not done so already – although based largely on the counselling and therapy end of the helping professions, it has much of relevance to coaches.

The seven eyes of the original refer to the client, the practitioner/supervisee, the supervisor, the interactions between client and practitioner, between practitioner and supervisor, between client supervisor (these are imagined), and the context. Hawkins and Shohet draw circles within circles to represent these seven perspectives and the diagram vaguely resembles eyeballs.

I develop the model to include the client system, to consider the contexts that belong to each party as well as the overall context, and to show aspects of the interactions and underlying dynamics in more detail (see Figure 6.1). This enhanced framework captures the elements of the system within which client, practitioner and supervisor function.

This does mean, of course, that the framework is a very thorough checklist so keep in mind that, as with the stages and process, I do not intend that you concentrate on everything. Experience will guide you but the framework can be used to check that nothing significant is overlooked.

Contexts, people, interactions and dynamics

You will see that there are four main columns – contexts, people, interactions and dynamics. Each of these four columns is sub-divided. On the far left is the overall context within which the practice occurs, such as the national culture, economic pressures, social expectations, legal constraints, and so on. Although these apply to all parties, the impact of various factors on the various parties may of course be quite different. Closely associated with overall context are the specific contexts that apply to each party – for the client this might be a family or work environment, which may or may not be shared by the client contact(s); for the coach and supervisor, this might incorporate their respective professional bodies, and perhaps an organization that is the 'buyer' of the coaching or supervision provision.

Next come the people involved, in terms of their roles and their personal characteristics. Roles might include being a colleague, manager, friend,

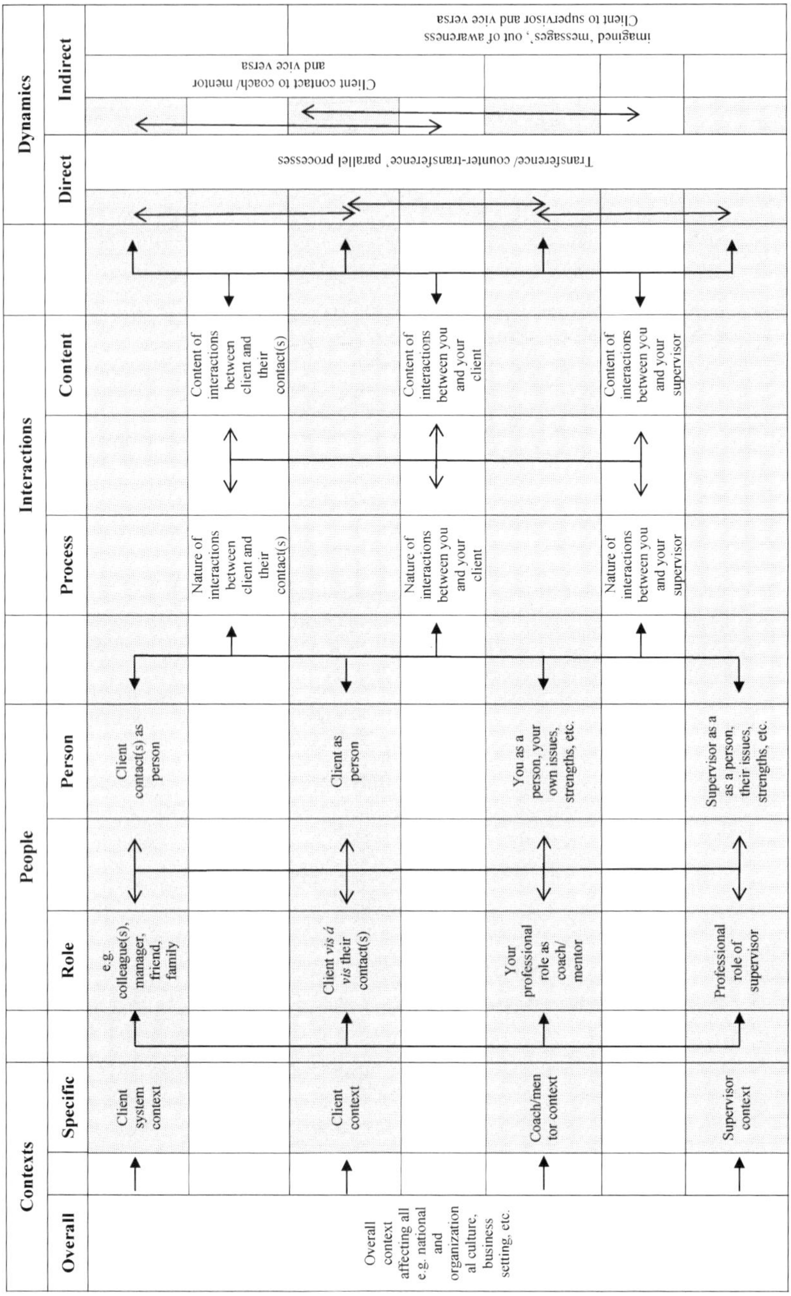

Contexts		People		Interactions		Dynamics	
Overall	Specific	Role	Person	Process	Content	Direct	Indirect
Overall context affecting all e.g. national and organizational culture, business setting, etc.	Client system context	e.g. colleague(s), manager, friend, family	Client contact(s) as person	Nature of interactions between client and their contact(s)	Content of interactions between client and their contact(s)	Transference/counter-transference, parallel processes	Client contact to coach/mentor and vice versa
	Client context	Client *vis à vis* their contact(s)	Client as person				Client to supervisor and vice versa; imagined 'messages', out of awareness
	Coach/mentor context	Your professional role as coach/mentor	You as a person, your own issues, strengths, etc.	Nature of interactions between you and your client	Content of interactions between you and your client		
	Supervisor context	Professional role of supervisor	Supervisor as a person, their issues, strengths, etc.	Nature of interactions between you and your supervisor	Content of interactions between you and your supervisor		

Figure 6.1 Reflecting systemically

relative for the client contact, employee, manager friend, relative for the client, coach as the role of the coach and, of course, supervisor as the role of the supervisor. Personal characteristics are the 'personalities' involved – in other words, the issues, skills and resources that each party brings to the situation.

The third pair of columns is about the interactions between client contact and client, client and coach, coach and supervisor. There is the content, which may be biased towards either their roles or their personal characteristics, and the process of the interactions, such as the levels of questioning, supporting and challenging, how the relationship is functioning, and whether this is appropriate in terms of the respective roles, issues and content.

Finally, we can reflect on the dynamics. For the direct dynamics between client contact(s) and client, client and coach, and coach and supervisor, key aspects to reflect on are whether parallel processes (Searles 1955) are in operation, effectively or not, whether there exists symbiosis, transference, countertransference, etc. The indirect dynamics are those 'imaginary' interactions where the client contact 'speaks' to the coach (or vice versa) or the client 'signals' to the supervisor (again, or vice versa).

Permutations

Each of the segments in Figure 6.1 can of course be reflected upon in isolation. Each will almost certainly generate useful insights in this way. However, the elements are all interlinked within a system. For example, the overall context may interact with the specific contexts of two of the parties, impacting on their roles which may well be in conflict with their persona, leading to overly cautious interactions focused on a limited range of content, with repeating patterns between the client and their contact and the supervisor with the coach, which just happen to be conveyed below the level of awareness from the client to the supervisor.

> *William, Freddie and Sam*
> Supervisor William was working with coach Freddie who had brought a piece of work with client Sam. Sam had been talking about difficulties in implementing an action plan because of lack of family support – Sam's partner wanted Sam to spend less time studying outside working hours while Sam was attending evening classes for accountancy.
>
> Freddie had recognized that there were significant context differences in operation – Sam was situated within a family context plus a working context as an employee in a job that Sam regarded as

simply a necessary evil in order to pay the bills – whereas Freddie had little family contact and was thoroughly committed to, and got much satisfaction from, being a coaching professional.

In terms of the overall context, Freddie felt part of the professional class and had parents and grandparents who had also been professionals, whereas Sam's origins were more working class, although Sam's aspirations were clearly focused on becoming a professional.

During the supervision, William recognized a sense of wanting to encourage Sam to continue to study regardless of family opposition. It was as if Sam were there with William – in terms of parallel process, William was behaving encouragingly towards Freddie and hence increasing the likelihood that Freddie would in turn encourage Sam towards a specific course of action.

William recognized that this was prompted in part by having experienced similar context factors as Sam – William had moved from working class to being a professional. Freddie was an advanced supervisee so William opted to analyse these dynamics and the impact of contexts overtly as part of the supervision.

This enabled Freddie to understand how context factors were feeding through and subtly influencing the interactions during the work with Sam. With this awareness, Freddie could ensure that Sam was prompted to consider different perspectives and, most importantly, make the decision without being influenced by the coach or indirectly by the supervisor.

Note that a similar result might have been attained wherever in the framework the analysis started. In this case, the parallel process within the dynamics prompted the supervisor to consider the context. An alternative example might have arisen if the supervisor had started with consideration of the roles of the client, coach and supervisor. This might have prompted an examination of the content of the interactions, which might have yielded evidence of the coach's opinions. Tracking the source of these opinions would have led back to the coach's personal issues and hence to both specific and overall context as the sources of the opinions (overall context) and the belief that such opinions had no place within the relationship (specific context – professional behaviour expectations).

I have already mentioned that each element of the framework can be examined in its own right. However, the purpose of the model is to encourage reflection on the system, so the arrows become the focus of attention. Each operates in two directions and can also be considered as part of a sequence of inter-connecting arrows.

The remainder of this chapter consists of a sequence of activities, with some that focus on specific elements and others that concentrate on how elements influence each other within the 'system'.

For the first series of activities, we commence with the People column so you can position yourself. We then prompt you to consider the overall and specific contexts, and after that the interactions and finally the dynamics.

Activity 6.1   Reflecting on the people and their roles

Use the prompts to review who you are professionally, who are your typical clients (or concentrate on each client in turn), your client contacts and your supervision arrangements.

Coach (myself)

- What is the nature of my professional role?
- What kind of coaching work do I undertake?
- How do I describe my services to potential clients?
- How do I differentiate myself from other professionals?
- Which clients or which client issues would I *not* work with?

Client

- What is the client's role (or roles), e.g. employee, manager, sportsperson, parent, professional, etc.?
- How significant are the client roles to the work we will do together?
- What is the relationship between my role and those of the client(s)?
- What is the nature of the role responsibilities held by the client(s)? How familiar do I need to be with such responsibilities?
- How might the client role requirements conflict or support the work we do together?

Client contacts

- What are the roles of people the client is in contact with, e.g. manager(s) of client, subordinates, colleagues, family, friends, customers, etc.?
- Which of these roles are significant in our work together?
- What is the nature of the roles of client contacts? How familiar do I need to be with this?
- How might the roles and responsibilities of client contacts impact on the client? And on what the client presents in the coaching sessions?
- How familiar with client contact roles is the client? How familiar does the client need to be?

Supervisor

- What is the nature of the supervisory role?
- What kind of supervision do I experience?

- What kind (and level) of supervision do I require?
- How does the supervision I get fit my client workload and profile?
- What might I avoid taking to a specific supervisor? Why? What else do I do about such matters?

Activity 6.2   Reflecting on the people and their personal characteristics

Coach

- What issues do I have that might affect my practice? What do I need to do about these to ensure my professionalism?
- What are my values and beliefs about coaching? And about supervision?
- What are my values and beliefs about clients? And about client contacts?
- What is my personality type (using whatever psychological framework I am familiar with – and maybe more than one)?
- What do I get out of being a coach?

Client

- What is my diagnosis of the client?
- What issues does the client have that might affect our work together? Which of these should be dealt with directly as part of our work?
- What needs to be done about client issues that are outside our coaching remit?
- What is the client's personality type? How might this match or contrast with my own?
- What do I need to pay particular attention to with this client?

Client contacts

- What are my diagnoses of the various client contacts? How reliable are these diagnoses (assuming they are based on information provided by the client rather than direct observation)?
- How might my conclusions about client contacts have been 'contaminated' by the client's own reactions?
- What are the client contact personality types? What might the implications of this be for their contact with the client?
- What issues might arise that are outside our coaching contract? What do I need to do about these? What do I need to prompt the client to do (if anything)?
- What do I need to pay particular attention to in terms of these client contacts?

Supervisor

- What personal or professional issues do I think my supervisor has? What can I do to ensure these do not have a detrimental impact on my supervision?

- What values and beliefs does my supervisor exhibit towards coaching? Towards the type of coaching I undertake?
- What values and beliefs does my supervisor exhibit towards my clients? Towards the typical issues brought by my clients?
- What is my supervisor's personality type? How does this match or contrast with my own?
- What does my supervisor appear to get out of being a supervisor?

Activity 6.3   Reflecting on the interplay between roles and personal characteristics

Review your responses in Activities 6.1 and 6.2 to identify areas of congruence and of potential conflict between both roles and personal characteristics, i.e. consider the 'vertical' arrows:

- How well aligned are the roles?
- Where might role conflicts arise?
- Are there any dual roles, such as being coach of a colleague, or supervisee of someone who is also the line manager?
- Are 'personality clashes' likely?
- Could it become too 'cosy' due to shared personal attributes?

Review your responses for each pair of role/personal aspects, i.e. the horizontal arrows:

- How might personal characteristics affect the ways in which roles are undertaken?
- How might role requirements and boundaries restrict the application of the full range of human characteristics?
- How might each role stimulate personal growth and development?
- Are there any patterns of which 'type' of person is drawn to which role? Is this appropriate?
- Have any of the roles been designed in a way that 'invites' a particular personality type? Is this appropriate?

Activity 6.4   Reflecting on specific contexts

Coach context (my own)

- Within what context am I practising, e.g. organizational scheme, internal or external, freelance?
- What is the status of my practice, e.g. full-time coach, coaching alongside another role?
- Within what field am I practising, e.g. sports, life, business, executive, etc.? What contextual implications are there?

- What codes of professional practice and ethics are relevant to my work?
- What professional associations are relevant to my practice? Am I/should I be a member? What are the implications of membership/non-membership?

Client context

- What is the status of the client, e.g. employed, self-employed, unemployed, student, refugee, entrepreneur, manager, parent, etc.?
- What is the context for the client, e.g. organization, family, team, committee, school, small company, charity, etc.?
- What constraints does the client's context impose on them, e.g. employee obligations, family expectations, etc.?
- What professional bodies, trade unions, interest groups, etc. have an impact on the client? In what ways?
- What professional norms, codes of practice or similar requirements apply to the client, e.g. non-discriminatory, health and safety, environmental, corporate rules, social expectations, etc.?

Client contact context

- What is the context for the client contact(s), e.g. family, friends, workplace, school, etc.?
- Is the contact context different from the client context? What are the implications of difference? Of sameness?
- What constraints does the context impose on client contacts, e.g. corporate norms, family expectations, society norms, business rules, etc.?
- What professional bodies, trade unions, interest groups, etc. have an impact on the client contacts? In what ways?
- What is the place of coaching within the context of the client contacts? How do I need to take this into account?

Supervisor context

- Within what context is my supervisor operating, e.g. independent, employed, paid for by organization, etc.?
- Within what fields is my supervisor functioning, e.g. supervision of sports coaches, community mentors, life coaches, business mentors, etc.?
- What professional associations are relevant to my supervisor? Is/should the supervisor be a member? What are the implications of membership/non-membership?
- What codes of professional practice and ethics are relevant to the supervision?
- What is the professional context of my supervisor, e.g. contact with supervisory colleagues, their own supervision arrangements, etc.?

Activity 6.5   Reflecting on the overall context

- What is the immediate context for my practice, e.g. working independently within an organizational or scheme setting, working with families, educational establishments, social work departments, etc.?
- How broadly does the context extend, e.g. one family, one company, one school, etc. or one geographical area, one racial group, one nation, or multinationally or spanning various professions?
- How clearly can I define the boundaries of the context? Or are the boundaries vague or subject to change?
- How aligned are the context boundaries for me, the client and their contexts, and my supervisor? What implications are there for different boundaries? For similar boundaries?
- How easy is it for me to maintain the overall boundaries? Might broader factors intrude and have an impact on my work?
- Does the client need support to deal with the impact of the context? Does the client need to be challenged over accepting limitations within the context?

Activity 6.6   Reflecting on the interplay between overall and specific contexts

A useful checklist for aspects of context is **SPECTRE** (Hay 2000) – social, political, economic, competitive, technological, regulatory and environmental. Use the SPECTRE prompts below (or any alternative checklist you are familiar with) to reflect on the overall context of your practice and how this might impact upon the various parties. This may be an organizational or scheme setting, a national or international context, a family, residential home, prison, hospital or any other context.

Overall context	Client system	Client	Coach	Supervisor
social e.g. education, family patterns, health, working patterns, retirement patterns				
political e.g. national government, local government, other countries, political changes, political unrest, political party activities				
economic e.g. cost of living, interest rates, mortgages, loans, international monetary factors, purchasing patterns				

competitive e.g. competition within sector, new products or services, impact on consumers, state of markets, marketing strategies				
technological e.g. new technology, technological advances, home and business impact, resources needed, resources created				
regulatory e.g. laws, legal requirements for organizations and individuals, product and service legislation, employment practices				
environmental e.g. environmental changes, environmental stewardship, world's resources, pollution, nature of local environment				

Activity 6.7   Reflecting on interactions

Previous chapters have contained many suggestions for analysing the processes of your interactions so I will not repeat them here. Instead, I will concentrate on prompts for reflecting on the content, and how this relates to the other elements of the 'system':

- What are typical issues raised by my clients?
- Do most clients raise similar issues or is there wide variation between different clients?
- How might the content raised be related to the role(s) of the clients and/or their contacts?
- How might the content raised be influenced by personality factors, styles, etc.?
- What significant issues are typically not raised by my clients? Are they unaware of these issues or reluctant to talk to me about them?
- What are the typical issues that I take to supervision? Are there repeating patterns? If so, how will I resolve these?
- Are there issues I prefer not to take to supervision? Why? What am I doing to ensure I get adequate supervision on issues I would rather ignore?
- What impact do the contexts (mine, the client's, the supervisor's, and overall) have on the content addressed during my coaching and reflection or supervision sessions? What might I need to discuss that is currently being 'overlooked'?

Activity 6.8   Reflecting on dynamics

Direct dynamics between client and their context, between coach and client, and between supervisor and coach, can be analysed in terms of parallel processes (see Chapter 5 and Activity 5.2) and transference and countertransference (see Chapter 1 and Activity 1.3).

The indirect dynamics may occur between client system and coach and between client and supervisor. Prompts for reflecting on these are shown in the followings:

Coach and client system

- Is there, or has there been, any contact between the client system and the coach or is it all via the client?
- What do I imagine that the client contacts might say to me if they could?
- What would I like to say (or do) to the client contacts? What might have prompted my reactions?
- How will I bring any imagined dynamics into awareness – for myself and for my client?
- How will I resolve, eliminate, or make use of any such indirect dynamics?

Client and supervisor

- Is there, or has there been, any contact between client and supervisor? What is/was the nature of this contact?
- How might such contact affect my practice with the client?
- How might such contact affect the supervisory relationship? And the supervision process?
- Do I have any fantasies about hidden dynamics between my client and my supervisor? What is the element of reality within such fantasies?
- How will I make such dynamics part of the content of my supervision? How will I reflect on them with my supervisor?

Activity 6.9   Reflecting on the interplay across the system

Track the various 'pathways' from overall context through to indirect dynamics. For example, consider how a corporate setting for the client contacts impacts on the role of the coach, such that interactions are constrained because the supervisor knows more about the client's role than the coach does. Or how a stressed client might unwittingly be 'signalling' a need for management intervention in their workload by raising issues that you take to supervision – and the supervisor recognizes the client context is not being managed in line with company policy?

- Within the 'pathways' are there similarities in terms of patterns of connections? Do these relate to all of my clients, particular types of clients, specific issues raised, or some other factor?

- What additional insights become available to me when I track the system in the opposite direction – from indirect dynamics (the music behind the words) back through to the various contexts the stakeholders operate within?

7   Contracting and Boundaries

I have introduced a number of theories and frameworks so will now extend these to provide details of some of the more general models that apply across the processes of reflection and supervision. In this chapter, I offer an overview of contracting and consideration of boundaries. To me, contracting is an essential skill and also a way of working with another person that invites and encourages them to stay in the here-and-now and take responsibility for their own actions. This chapter provides a classification of levels as well as various ways to reflect on multi-party contracts in a range of situations. There is also material on the ethical dimensions of our professional practices and a detailed consideration of the ways that metaphors impact on our lives.

Why contract?

I've made several mentions of contracting in previous chapters. I believe that contracting is the key to effective coaching and supervision – good contracting ensures that those involved share the same idea of the purpose of the relationship and the current session, that the respective roles and responsibilities are made explicit, and that responsibility is shared for the forthcoming process. Having a clear contract also creates a relationship in which honesty and openness are encouraged and the boundaries are clarified and agreed. This means that potential problems can be identified at an early stage and the contract can include ways of dealing with them if they still arise.

Contracts may be written or verbal. Although the term 'contract' has a legal meaning, it is also customarily applied to any ways in which two or more parties come to an agreement. Thus, although we hope that it will never be tested in a court of law, the contract we agree with a client (or supervisee) should be regarded as just as important.

One-to-one contracts

The most straightforward contracting involves just the coach and the client. We'll look later at what happens for supervision or peer reflection, where there are at least three parties involved (client, coach, supervisor) and also at multi-party contracts such as for organizational schemes.

An initial framework for reflection consists of thinking about contracting at three levels: procedural, professional and psychological. The procedural level consists of the administrative routines, such as how often, where and for how long will we meet, what documentation will be kept, what happens if one of us needs to cancel an appointment. The professional level is about what type of coaching is involved, and what are the boundaries of the relationship, including confidentiality agreements and the fact that there will be no therapy. The psychological level refers to what might happen out of awareness, what should we pay overt attention to, such as potential dependency issues or dual relationships.

Activity 7.1 Reflecting on a one-to-one contract

For each client, use the following checklist to review your overall contract, as it was initially established – identify any gaps and plan to check back on these with your client. Has your contract addressed the following elements?

Procedural

- How long is the relationship likely to last?
- What frequency of meetings?
- Where we will meet? (Will this vary?)
- What notes will be kept? By whom? Where will they be kept? Are they accessible to others?
- What is the procedure if one of us needs to cancel a session? How will we re-arrange?
- Do either of us have 'gate-keepers' who take messages or manage our diaries? If so, what will they be told about our relationship?

Professional

- What is the nature of the coaching (traditional, developmental, business, life, etc.)?
- Are we both fully in agreement with that?
- Have we checked we both have the same understanding of what we mean?
- What are the boundaries to our relationship?
- What issues should the client take elsewhere?
- How will we know when issues are outside our agreed boundaries?
- What referral options are we aware of (e.g. therapist, counsellor, business adviser, accountant, etc.)?
- What are the expected outcomes from working together?
- Are we satisfied that the professional level of the contract is within our competence?
- Have we specified what is *outside* the contract, such as coach acting on behalf of the client, or discussing client's performance with a line manager?

Psychological

- What aspects have we brought into awareness that might otherwise have influenced under the surface?
- Have we both been open about any anxieties or concerns we have?
- Have we considered how either of us might unwittingly sabotage our relationship?
- Have we planned how to recover trust if something does go wrong?
- Have we addressed the potential dependency issues? The possibility that the client may feel overwhelmed? Or rebellious?
- What ground rules have we agreed to ensure that either one of us will feel comfortable enough to raise any issues with our relationship?
- If we were to play psychological games, what might the dynamics be? How can we avoid games?

Three-cornered contracting

We often need to contract with another party as well as the client, such as an organization that is paying for our services. There may also be implicit stakeholders such as the client's line manager, or the pupils when our client is a teacher. The three-cornered contract, a concept introduced originally by Fanita English (1975) and extended by me (Hay 1996) gives us a simple diagram to illustrate the coach, client and organization dynamic (Figure 7.1). You can consider the three levels of the contract for the three sides of the triangle.

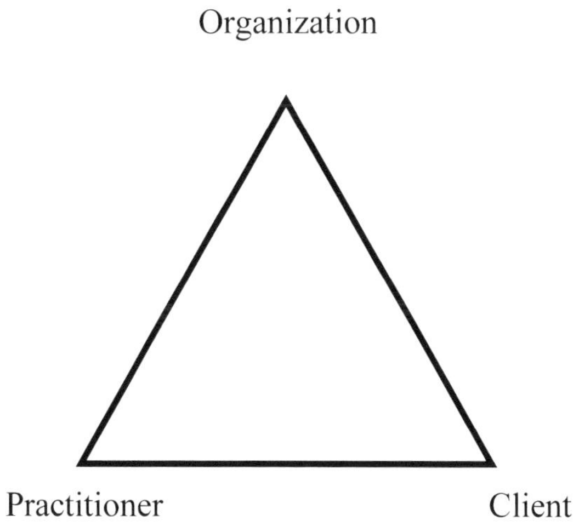

Organization

Practitioner   Client

Figure 7.1 The three-cornered contract

Elizabeth

I can recall being brought in by a personnel director – I'll call her Elizabeth – to provide coaching for her. As we clarified the contract, it became clear that she wished to work on whether or not to stay with the organization. She had a young child and was struggling with maternal instincts versus career orientation. She also advised me that the organization would be paying for the coaching and that I should send my invoices to her.

This meant that I needed a three-cornered contract. Whereas normally Elizabeth, as personnel director, might have been the official representative of the organization, I did not feel that this was appropriate when the service being purchased contained an element of significant personal benefit to her. I therefore explained the notion of three-cornered contracting and asked that her manager become the third party who would represent the interests of the organization. He agreed and confirmed that it was acceptable for me to spend time helping Elizabeth decide whether or not to leave the organization. (He pointed out, in fact, that the organization would be better off if she left than if she stayed but continued to lack motivation because the maternal versus career conflict was still unresolved.) He also confirmed that the usual agreement about confidentiality could apply and that he would expect information about our coaching discussions to come only from Elizabeth – I would not be expected to alert him if she began planning her exit strategy.

Activity 7.2   Contracting and the organization

We can add another dimension to the prompts in Activity 7.1.

What *procedural* arrangements does the organization expect?

- Has the organization specified an overall time period for the relationship, the frequency of meetings, the length of sessions?
- Does the organization expect to have sight of any documentation? Are reports required, including client feedback about the coach?

What *professional* expectations does the organization have?

- What type of coaching is intended?
- What are the boundaries set by the organization (related to current job only, personal circumstances, career advancement, changing employer, etc.)?
- What referral options are provided by the organization (e.g. counselling scheme, employee assistance programme)?
- What other support is available (e.g. educational sponsorship, training courses, shadowing options)?

What *psychological* undercurrents might there be?

- Unspoken expectations that the coach is there to 'mould' the client to suit the needs of the organization?
- Client fears about the coach reporting on them to the organization?
- Organization using coaching as a last resort or so they can justify sacking the client?
- Unrealistic expectations of what coaching can achieve?

Four-cornered contract

The three-cornered contract becomes more complex when we consider other potential stakeholders (Figure 7.2). For instance, there will often be a line manager of the client. Although this person may not be directly involved in the coaching arrangements, a line manager will still have an impact on the coaching. Line managers are usually the ones to evaluate performance, they may take a lot of convincing before they drop the paranoid belief that their subordinates use coaching sessions to complain about managers, and they may also generate extra tasks that make it hard for clients to keep appointments. On the other hand, they can provide valuable developmental support to your clients provided they understand the nature of the coaching.

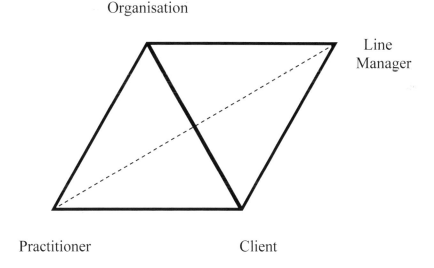

Figure 7.2 The four-cornered contract

When reflecting on the impact of a client's line manager, it may help to review first the three-cornered contract of organization, manager and client/ employee. In this, the organization and client have a contract that basically says: client/employee does a job and organization pays them to do so. (This is of course underpinned by the contract of employment.) A similar contract exists between the organization and the line manager – do the job and get paid. The significant element here is that the manager's contract includes the responsibility for ensuring the client/employee fulfils their own contract with the organization.

Activity 7.3 Contracting and the line manager

The line manager may impact on the coaching relationship in several ways: additional prompts for reflecting on this are as follows:

Procedurally

- How does the line manager react to the client being absent from work for coaching sessions?
- Does the manager accept this, resent it but put up with it, or allocate urgent tasks so the client has to cancel sessions?

Professionally

- Does the manager understand how the coaching is a different process to that of management?
- Does the manager accept that coaching is confidential or demand to know the details, from the client/employee or the coach?
- Does the manager recognize that the coach will not deal with management issues on behalf of the manager – in other words, that the coach will not do the line manager's job?

Psychologically

- Is the manager worrying that the coach is listening to the client/employee complain about the manager?
- Is the manager going through the motions as expected by the organization while giving off signals of feeling that the client is betraying the manager by talking to someone else?

Identify any potential problems and consider how you might work with clients who are also employees, so that such clients can 'manage' the line manager dimension. See also Activity 7.5   for some prompts you could apply to the line manager.

Multi-party contracting

As if four parties were not complicated enough, we may be working in circumstances where there are several stakeholders. For example, you as coach may be employed by a consultancy that has contracted with your client's organization. Or you may be contributing to a coaching scheme being run for a consortium of organizations. Figure 7.3 shows how this looks if you and the client each have line managers.

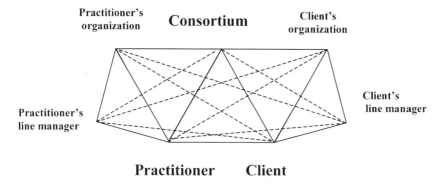

Figure 7.3 Multi-party contracting – consortium

An alternative shown in Figure 7.4, shows similar complexity when you are coaching a client such as a teacher.

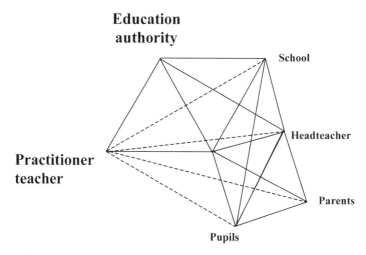

Figure 7.4 Multi-party contracting – educational context

Although the above shows what appear to be 'silent' stakeholders, they will still have expectations that will influence your work with the client.

Activity 7.4   Stakeholder prompts

For each additional party, consider the following prompts:

- Do the client and I know what the expectations of this stakeholder are?
- What have we done to reflect these in our own contract?
- What might we need to do to deal with any unrealistic expectations?
- What might happen if we ignore this stakeholder's expectations?

Activity 7.5   Professional associations as stakeholder

One of the implicit stakeholders will be whatever professional association(s) you belong to. As you consider the prompts in Activity 7.5, you might also reflect on the following:

- What have I told the client about the expectations of my professional association?
- How might the professional standards of that association impact on my work with this client? Have I taken that into account?
- What aspects of the association's code of ethics have relevance to work with this client?
- Have I advised the client about the code of ethics and how to register a complaint against me?
- Is there more than one professional association that might be relevant to my work with this client?

Psychological distances

An interesting insight into the psychological level of contracts involving three or more parties can be obtained via the concept of **psychological distance** (Micholt 1992; Hay 1996). This is the felt, or fantasized, distance between parties. Are they close or distant? Using the three-cornered triangle, we can represent different psychological distances by varying the lengths of the sides, as shown in Figure 7.5.

Figure 7.5(a) shows a relationship where the coach and client are close and the organization is at a distance. This typically happens when the coach has over-identified with the client (and forgotten who is paying for the coaching), and/or when the client presents as a victim of organizational politics, and/or when the organization is demonstrating little real interest in the coaching scheme.

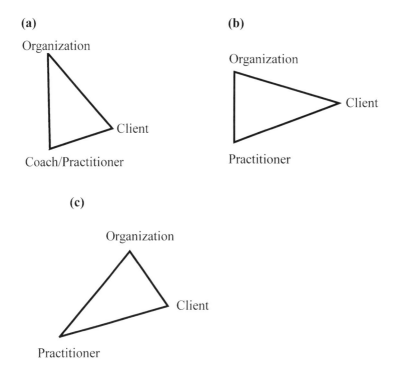

Figure 7.5 Psychological distances

When you reflect on this, take note that the potential consequences of continuing with this pattern of psychological distances include the risk of the organization dispensing with your services. It may also mean that you are keeping the client in victim mode instead of enabling them to take responsibility for their own actions.

Figure 7.5(b) illustrates the distances when the coach aligns with the organization and aims to 'sort out' the client – who feels as if impaled on the sharp end. This may occur when the coach is an employee of the organization, and/or when clients present in ways that makes it hard to like them, and/or when coaching schemes require that coaches assess clients and holds coaches responsible for client progress.

Again, you might reflect on possible outcomes, such as having a rebellious client who refuses to co-operate or the organization deciding that you've failed as a coach.

Figure 7.5(c) shows the final variation, with the client and the organization appearing to collude so the coach feels left out. This pattern is less common and arises when an organization is running coaching because someone senior decided it was a good idea – but where line managers regard it as a waste of time. Clients pick up their manager's views and respond by 'going through the motions'.

The danger with this pattern is that the coach reacts inappropriately to the client's cynicism and either gives up trying or becomes too pushy. Either way, the coach then reinforces the client's (and the line manager's) low opinion of coaching.

If you work with clients who make their own arrangements with no other stakeholder having any involvement or interest in the coaching, you will not need to consider psychological distances. However, even where the client is self-funding, it can still be useful to reflect on who else might be aware of the coaching or might notice any changes in the client. For example, clients working within organizations who seek coaching related to current performance may need to take into account the impact on their line manager; those asking for personal coaching may need to consider family reactions; and those considering career development may need to take account of the expectations of potential recruiters. It can be useful, therefore, to reflect on psychological distances between implicit as well as explicit stakeholders.

Activity 7.6   Psychological distances

For a specific client, list all stakeholders and/or implicit stakeholders. Sketch a series of three-cornered contracts for you in combination with the client and each stakeholder in turn. Do these intuitively to see what shapes emerge.

Review each 'stakeholder triangle' in turn, reflecting on the following:

1   How close do you feel to the client compared to the other stakeholder?
2   How might these levels of closeness be exhibited in your behaviour?
3   How close do you think the client feels to you compared to the other stakeholder?
4   What is it about the client's behaviour that may be prompting you to this interpretation?
5   What is your speculation about how the third party might perceive the relationship between you and the client?
6   What might the client have said or done to prompt your speculation?
7   What actions, if any, might you need to initiate in order to achieve balanced psychological distances?
8   What might you prompt the client to consider to avoid any imbalance?

Contracting for reflection with colleagues

The benefits of contracting are not restricted to coach and client relation-ships. Clear contracting with colleagues will ensure that you stay focused on reflecting and avoid the trap of giving each other advice. It will also help you manage the process jointly, especially as you each switch roles from super-visor to supervisee. You can also make sure that the contract is worded in such a way that it reinforces your own responsibility for your own clients. Reflec-tion colleagues may need to challenge you if you seem unaware of any un-helpful practice on your part – but they must still recognize the boundaries of clients being yours and not theirs. To reinforce this, the contract should also make clear the need to maintain confidentiality relating to your clients, so that your reflection colleagues have no need to know who the clients are.

Activity 7.7   Contracting for peer supervision

This is similar to Activity 7.1 with the questions tailored instead to provide the basis for contracting to reflect on each other's work rather than simply reviewing your own contracting with a client. Hence, the prompts become as follows:

Procedural

- When, where, how often and for how long each time will we meet?
- How will we share out the time in each session (equal shares and we each present a case; we each present intermittently when we feel the need; we operate a rota as one session is too short for all of us)?
- What happens about cancellations (is the group big enough to operate if we don't all turn up; shall we be deemed to have left the group if we miss a number of consecutive sessions; do we expect to provide explanations for absences)?

Professional

- Do we share the same understanding of what is involved in reflection and peer supervision?
- What are the boundaries to our relationship?
- How will we handle things when we realise that personal issues need ad-dressing (especially when the group recognizes this and the individual coach does not)?
- What is our commitment to confidentiality?
- What will we do if we believe that one of us is behaving unethically?
- What will we tell our clients about this process of peer reflection?
- What have we specified as being *outside* the contract?

Psychological

- What ground rules do we want to establish to encourage openness and trust?
- How will we deal with issues of shame regarding sharing our 'mistakes' with colleagues?
- How will we avoid competitiveness (including competing to be *more* open, to have made a *bigger* mistake)?
- How will we handle conflict while ensuring we don't restrict ourselves to 'nice' feedback?

Contracting with a supervisor

The frameworks already described, such as the procedural, professional and psychological levels, stakeholder involvements and psychological distances are, of course, just as relevant when you contract with a supervisor. We can encapsulate much of this via the prompts in Activity 7.9 at the end of this chapter. However, there are some additional considerations that are worth reviewing before you go on to that.

Client as stakeholder

Contracting with a supervisor will automatically mean there are at least three stakeholders – supervisor, supervisee and client. The supervisor–client dimension will be implicit in that they have no direct contact with each other (except on occasions when line supervision is being done). However, it will still be highly significant.

I was once audio-taping a session with someone who knew who my current supervisor was and who had previously been trained by him. In the midst of our work, after an intervention by me that seemed to work well, the client turned directly towards the tape recorder and said, 'Did you hear that, Archie? Wasn't it good?' So much for my belief that only myself and the client were in this interaction.

In Chapter 6, I borrowed from Hawkins and Shohet (2000) to propose that the implicit dynamics between supervisor and client are an area for review. Careful contracting can help to minimize any negative impact on the work with the client.

A key concept here is psychological distance. How can you maintain an equilateral triangle, so that neither supervisor nor supervisee feels closer to the client than to each other, or indeed further away? Check out factors such as whether there are any clients that you don't take to supervision. Is this really because the work is straightforward or might you be 'hiding' the client, not wanting to share a particular client with your supervisor? Are you perhaps fantasizing that talking about this client will somehow spoil the coach/client relationship?

Likewise, are there clients you omit from supervision because you are 'ashamed' of them or of your apparent lack of competence when with them? Are you trying to maintain closeness with your supervisor by censoring out any clients that might give the supervisor a poor impression of you?

Do you suspect that your supervisor has a better understanding of any of your clients than you have? Might this lead you to feel 'left out' psychologically? Or do you disagree with your supervisor about how to work with any of your clients? Might this lead you to feel resentful of your supervisor *or* to relate to closely to such a client in an effort to prove yourself right?

Professional associations as stakeholders

I mentioned earlier in this chapter that you may have to take into account the expectations of your professional association. Once you engage with a supervisor, this aspect becomes even more significant, especially as the two of you may belong to different associations. Consider how familiar your supervisor is with your codes of professional practices and ethics. Can these aspects realistically form part of the supervision process? In other words, how much of the normative element of supervision will be included?

How familiar are you with your supervisor's codes of professional practices and ethics? How will these impact on the supervision? Are your supervisor's codes compatible with those that apply to you? Might your supervisor have expectations that are out of line with your normal practice? How will the two of you deal with any differing expectations?

The three Rs of supervision

An easy checklist that I use for the start of each piece of supervision, and that can also be applied as an overall framework, is to think of the three Rs – in this case, *results, relationship* and *responsibility*.

- *Results* are what do you, the supervisee, want to achieve in the timeslot? Do you want to clarify your thinking, analyse an intervention, identify options for the future? From a supervisor's point of view, I will be checking that what you want is realistic in the time available and at your level of experience, and that I am competent to supervise this piece of work.
- *Relationship* refers to how we will agree to work together for this piece of supervision. Do you want to be asked questions, allowed to talk,

reflected back to, prompted through a structured approach, provided with information, challenged into greater insight, supported with a difficult client, etc.?

• *Responsibility* is listed essentially as a reminder that the supervisor is responsible for providing 'good enough' supervision (the best the supervisor can do) and you as supervisee are responsible for deciding what to take from the supervision, how to perform in future and what decisions you make when next with the client.

Mary

When Mary first came for supervision, she needed prompting to articulate her thoughts against the three Rs. As she engaged more with the supervision process, she learned to judge what could realistically be achieved within the 20-minute sessions I customarily use. She began to split her supervisory needs down into manageable chunks, sometimes opting for an initial session to explore her thinking or her actual interventions, and then realizing that she could now identify her own options.

At other times, she analysed her interventions unaided and could then present this briefly so that most of the supervision time could be focused on exploring options. At yet other times, she arrived for supervision on how to implement options, having analysed her interventions *and* identified her own set of options *before* coming to supervision.

Now, Mary often begins her slot with a clearly offered contract along the lines of: 'I know that I am responsible for what I decide to do as a result of this supervision. I would like you to ask me questions and prompt me to apply specific theoretical frameworks so that I can bring into awareness what happened with a recent intervention that did not work as I'd hoped. I want awareness and understanding only for now as I'm confident that I will then be better placed to choose from a range of options. I'll come back for more supervision if that turns out not to be the case.'

Activity 7.8   Contracting with a supervisor

• *Professionally*, how do we view the role of the supervisor? What balance between formative, normative and supportive? Are our expectations in line or do we need some adjustments?

• What *procedural* arrangements will apply – when, where, how often, for how long will we meet, what payment arrangements, what cancellation arrangements, etc.?

- *Psychologically*, what might be outside our awareness and hence might sabotage our work together? What shall we do about that?
- How many *'corners'* do we have to our contracting?
- What other *stakeholders*, explicit and implicit, have an involvement with this supervision? What do we need to do about that?

Contracting and ethics

An alternative framework for reflecting on our contracting processes and the boundaries of our practice is to consider the specific ethical and professional practice implications. Two key considerations are competence and legality. Are we and the client(s) competent to make the contract? Do we have the necessary skills and does the client understand the nature of the relationship and is not simply accepting what we propose? Will we be operating within the law and, where appropriate, within organizational requirements? Any confidentiality clause will need to be balanced with the responsibility of the practitioner to report matters such as child abuse, fraud or theft, or other illegal acts.

In addition to these key elements, you might also reflect on factors such as financial or other gains. Clients can become temporarily dependent on their practitioners. You therefore need to ensure that you make no secondary gains from your work – such as being left money in a client's will, or being awarded work contracts within a client's organization on the recommendation of the client. Check also that you are not inadvertently taking advantage of any pre-existing relationships, such as using your managerial position to turn your employees into clients. You need to recognize that any prior role as a coach means you should not now become a consultant or trainer to the same clients and/or their team.

You will also need to recognize the limitations and avoid inappropriate dual relationship roles, such as being counsellor and coach at the same time, or family member and professional practitioner. At the same time, there needs to be an ongoing commitment to clients, so that you maintain your professional relationships in appropriate ways. This might be by providing on-going support and follow-up or by declining opportunities of further work that you suspect may only be made because the client is still operating within an earlier client/practitioner perspective.

There are also some more general professional considerations. Continuing professional development (CPD) is essential if you are to keep up to date with developments in your field and hence offer your clients the best possible practice. Respect for the profession is also important, so that you do not denigrate colleagues, do not 'poach' clients from them (although you will, of course, allow clients freedom of choice); and you will challenge colleagues if you believe they are acting unprofessionally or unethically.

You need to meet the legal requirements in your country of practice, such as obtaining professional indemnity insurance, observing data protection laws, etc. Your self-presentation must be based on honest statements about your competence and qualifications, so that you do not misrepresent yourself or advertise in ways that claim more than you can achieve. It is also poor practice to use the names of other professionals to enhance our own standing, such as by claiming we were trained by them when we merely attended their workshops but were not assessed by them.

Activity 7.9   Reflecting on ethics

- How do I know that the client is competent to make this contract? And is choosing to do so, with no coercion by other stakeholders?
- Are there any legal or organizational requirements to be taken into account? What will I do if the client tells me she or he is breaking the law?
- How will I ensure that I make no secondary gains from this client?
- Is there any pre-existing relationship that would conflict with me being this client's coach?
- Am I likely to become involved in any inappropriate dual roles?
- What ongoing or follow-up support might be appropriate? Am I in a position to provide such support?
- Is my CPD activity sufficiently targeted to benefit this client?
- Have I behaved appropriately towards any other coaches this client may have contacted?
- Have I advised this client of the availability of other coaches so the client can make a choice?
- Have I met best practice requirements such as professional insurance, data protection, etc. – even if they are not legal requirements in my professional role?
- Have I been strictly factual about how I describe myself professionally?

Ethical beliefs

When we offer professional services, we need to be aware of our own values and beliefs and how these might affect our practice. I 'borrow' here from NLP and TA to provide some prompts of beliefs that seem to me to be relevant for a coaching professional.

From NLP, several pre-suppositions might apply. First, that *everyone operates within their own unique map of the world*. We therefore need to respect diversity in all its forms. If we are unwilling to work with someone because we cannot accept aspects such as their cultural norms, racial characteristics, sexual preferences, etc., we are failing to be flexible enough. Next, we need to work on the basis that *people are not the same as their behaviours.* We need to be able to separate behaviours and identity. If we add the pre-supposition that *all behaviours have a positive intention* (albeit in the perpetrator's map of the world and not ours), we will be able to work respectfully with a broader range of clients. Finally, an assumption that *we cannot not communicate* means that we accept that any issues we have are likely to 'leak' to our clients. We need a commitment to deal with our own issues, both professionally and personally. This means that we need to receive regular coaching and supervision on how we do our work.

From a TA perspective, there are similar assumptions. We respect diversity as part of our intention to operate in *I'm OK, You're OK* mode. We separate behaviours and identity because we recognize that such behaviour results from early scripting – our aim is to help the clients *make new decisions* based on what they now know of the world. We deal with our own issues because we know that we, like all humans, will behave sometimes in script-bound ways and we do not want our clients to be impacted by our issues. We therefore obtain therapy and/or supervision to deal with the possibility of parallel processes. This can be illustrated by a story told about Gandhi. A woman travelled a very long way to bring her son to Gandhi, whom she asked to cure the boy of taking so much sugar. Gandhi told her to come back in three weeks time. She made the long journey again, only to have Gandhi simply say to the boy 'Stop taking sugar.' When asked why he could not have saved her the journey and said that three weeks ago, Gandhi replied, 'Three weeks ago I was taking sugar.'

Activity 7.10   Reflecting on beliefs

Review the NLP and TA pre-suppositions and assumptions and consider:

- Which of them do you relate to? Why?
- Which of them do you reject? Why?
- Which of them are you ambivalent about?

Check out with reflection colleagues to see how their beliefs compare with yours.

Identify other beliefs that are relevant and create your own ethical framework. Reflect regularly on how this framework influences your practice.

Metaphors and boundaries

Metaphors

A client announces that time is money and we wonder about their values. Another complains that management is out of touch and we know just what this means. A third refers to wanting to have their cake and eat it too, prompting us to wonder how realistic this might be. At no time do we consciously think about actual money, or management physically restraining their hands, nor do we envisage the client eating a real cake. Instead, we recognize these metaphors for what they are – a way of understanding one kind of thing in terms of another (Lakoff and Johnson 1980).

Metaphors add richness to our maps, enabling us to convey a lot of meaning in a few words. At the same time, some of our metaphors are representations of paradigms in which exist powerful but implicit boundaries. Again, the metaphors enable us to convey these boundaries in a few words. Put the two together and we create a map of the world that has much implicit meaning within it and clearly implied boundaries around it.

We operate by following numerous everyday metaphors and paradigms, generally without realizing we are doing so because so many of them are shared.

Prompted by Molden (1996), we can identify several other models of time in addition to money:

- a possession – *I haven't got enough time; we have all the time in the world*;
- a commodity – *There's never enough time*;
- an opponent or ally – *Time is against us; time is on our side*;
- a person – *Time waits for no-one; time is passing*.

Molden suggests that we could instead think of time as an investment, so that we focus on: planning how best to invest time; evaluating our gains from our use of time; building an investment portfolio comprising activities such as learning and developing, building relationships, enjoying life.

O'Connor (1998) provides examples related to leadership that conjure up some amusing imagery if you consider them literally: larger than life, on a pedestal, ahead of the field, hands-on, having the common touch, out of touch. Many organizations have ways of talking about different maps as if they equate to wars, with people using phrases such as: winning and losing, shooting down other's arguments, attacking the weak points, being right on target, gathering ammunition. And how often have you heard people accused of moving the goalposts; throwing out the baby with the bath water; letting the side down? Or had the advantages of being a high-flyer or star performer; operating on a level playing-field; getting all the ducks in a row?

We often use metaphors to define ourselves, creating *identity maps* that contain implicit limitations. At the professional level, we may consider ourselves to be a leader, follower or bystander – and maybe find it hard to switch roles when appropriate. Or perhaps we are a professional, such as an accountant, an engineer, a salesperson, which roles carry with them rules and responsibilities for how we perform our duties. Another option is to be a particular type of person – caring, quick-thinking, principled – and maybe we struggle when events conspire against us so that we are taken advantage of, get impatient, have to compromise.

Eric Berne (1961) and Claude Steiner (1974) went further and suggested the notion of lifescripts. Berne refers to our use of fairy stories – people unwittingly become characters such as Little Red Riding Hood, Robin Hood, Prince Charming or Cinderella. We may instead become one of the other players in such stories, especially if we have decided not to be too important. Having heard the story that seems to fit our experiences of the world at a young age (before the age of 7), we decide to be that character and then grow up with no conscious awareness of our decision. Berne also referred to Joseph Campbell (1973) who had identified that there are only a limited number of themes to fairy stories around the world, and that these also fit Greek myths.

'Cinderella' may well work hard for many years while her (or his – these are unisex) manager (wicked stepmother) and colleagues (ugly sisters) take all the credit – until one day a mentor (fairy godmother) ensures that Cinders gets to present at the annual conference (ball) and the senior manager (Prince) finally recognizes just how good Cinders is and promotes her/him (marries and takes to castle). Or Robin Hood may adopt a role as official or unofficial staff representative (outlaw) and spend time arguing (fighting) with a manager (Sheriff of Nottingham) on behalf of the workforce (peasants), both overtly through open attacks and covertly by awarding perks that are outside the rules – until one day the Chief Executive (King Richard) makes a visit and sees what has been happening and demotes the manager and promotes Robin.

The modern version of this lifescript process may well be that children choose TV programmes or films instead of fairy stories. Perhaps we will now have people who live like characters from *Star Trek*, no longer boldly going but leading through involvement, or being totally empathic, or operating very rationally and without emotions – the programme offers many choices.

When we are functioning as coaches it is important that we become aware of our own metaphors and paradigms so that we do not impose these unwittingly on our clients. It can also be useful to check out how our metaphors compare with those of our reflection colleagues and supervisor.

I have identified five elements that we can pay attention to once we recognize that we are operating within a metaphor or paradigm. First, what does the map *embody*? What is the main thrust of the content, what responses does it generate within the body? If it is a story, what happens, what is it about? Are there specific steps or stages within it, what might it prompt someone to do?

Next, what does it *encompass*? How far does this particular map extend, does it apply only to a specific event, to a person or role, to a period of time? Might it define your whole life or that of the organization? What are the limits or boundaries? Where does the metaphor break down, is there a better alternative map?

Then, what does it *entail*? Is there a sting in the tail, does it have elements that you would prefer were not there? What might happen because of it that would be unhelpful, how ecologically sound is it? What might you be over-looking when you focus on the main theme? Do you need to change the map?

Then consider how might, or should, it be *enriched*? How much is it locked into your own cultural or other set of paradigms? How could you make it richer by being open to other people's maps of the world? How could you extend it by weaving in metaphors and paradigms from other cultures?

Finally, how does, or could, it *empower*? What 'power' does the map provide, what positive developmental elements does it contain? What is the impact on you or others of operating within the map? How might you change it so that it becomes more empowering?

8 Psychological Underpinnings

I've made repeated references to the psychological level of the contract, and back in Chapter 3 I mentioned several other psychological aspects, such as discounting, symbiosis and parallel process. You'll have concluded by now, no doubt, that I think that the underlying psychology is important. Hence, this chapter will add some more ideas, with an emphasis on how the supervisory relationship might go wrong – plus, of course, suggestions on how to apply the models to create the best supervisory experience possible.

Psychological games

You may well be aware already that **games** are a key concept within transactional analysis. Berne's (1964) book entitled *Games People Play* was a bestseller in its time, although be warned that if you read it now, it may seem dated, sexist and confusing. Rather like a medical textbook, I think its success was due to the fact that the readers could identify themselves as having so many of the symptoms. However the book seems, the notion of psychological games is a fascinating one. It is also made even more accessible by the work of Karpman (1968) who identified that the dynamics are rather like a stage play, with people taking on roles as Victim, Rescuer or Persecutor and the excitement coming when one or more of them switched positions.

Examples within coaching are easy to spot. Take the client you play 'Yes but . . .' with – this client appears to be asking for your advice; you are invited into Rescuer and start suggesting what the client might do; the client gently knocks down all your suggestions with 'Yes but I couldn't do that because . . .'; eventually you get so frustrated with the client that you run out of patience and Persecute the client for being so negative – and the client trumps you by pointing out that you were not actually asked for any advice.

When it comes to supervision, games will still be played sometimes, however self-aware and reflective we become. It may help to recognize that a psychological game is actually a failed attempt at establishing closeness. When we can't achieve the open, trusting relationship that would lead to an exchange of positive strokes, we settle instead for negative strokes as being better than being ignored. Children all learn this lesson – the naughty ones get all the attention from the teacher. Without human attention, we may fail to develop properly; I mentioned in Chapter 5 how this happened to the orphans in Romania. Being stroked negatively, in spite of reinforcing unhealthy behaviour, will still meet our biological need for human recognition.

Games played in supervision

'Yes but's' full name is in fact 'Why don't you ... Yes, but ...'. Supervisees act in a Victim-like manner, not asking directly for help but instead giving out signals of helplessness, saying with a sigh that they just don't know what to do, or just sitting there not saying anything. Supervisors are thus tempted to Rescue, coming in with 'helpful' comments, which escalate into suggestions as the full impact of the supervisees' helplessness is felt. Supervisees may then Persecute by getting annoyed, or perhaps they seem eminently reasonable while pointing out that the supervisor is going outside the boundaries of the contract and behaving unprofessionally, or even unethically. A longer-term version of this game involves supervisees taking the supervisor's advice, implementing it, and coming back to complain bitterly about how bad the advice has turned out to be. At this point, the supervisees can blame the supervisor for any negative consequences. The supervisee may also tell others that it was a supervisor's suggestion they were following and they never really liked the idea anyway. Supervisors are left wondering how being helpful got them into such a mess.

Another potential supervision game is called Kick Me. In this, supervisees play Victim and keep doing things wrong. Supervisors are shining examples of patience and persist in giving positive feedback, even when it becomes very hard to find something associated with a supervisee that is worthy of positive strokes. ('Your eyes are a nice colour' has its limitations as a piece of supervisory feedback.) For a long as supervisors avoid giving constructive criticism, supervisees will continue to do things wrong. Eventually, the supervisors lose patience and give negative feedback – the problem is that their frustration means their comments come out sounding far more critical and impatient than intended. Supervisees then become visibly distressed and claim to be too upset to continue working, after which the supervisors feel they are to blame for upsetting the supervisees, so go back to positive comments only, run out of these and shift to a negative again, supervisees are again devastated, and so the dynamics bounce backwards and forwards.

Activity 8.1   Game-free supervision

The clues to game playing are that it is repetitive, predictable, familiar, has an ulterior level of communication, and leads to negative payoffs for all involved. The more times you answer yes to one of the following prompts, the more likely it is that you are engaging in a game. Use your awareness of this to decide how to behave differently before the game has got started.

Is it a game?

- Are there any repetitive patterns within your supervisory dynamics? Any actions, feelings or thoughts that you feel keep repeating, over and over?
- Are there times when you feel that the supervisory interactions have become predictable? Could an observer predict what is going to happen next?
- Do you get a sense of déjà vu, of here we go again, of why does this keep happening to me?
- Are there things you are not saying to your supervisor? Are you hiding your feelings, censoring your words, changing the subject?
- Do you sense that the supervisor is holding back, not saying something that might be said, protecting you from the supervisor's feedback?

What are the dynamics?

- Make notes on how the game starts. Who says or does what? How does the other party respond?
- What happens next? How much iteration is there? How many repetitions of the same dynamic before things seem to shift?
- How do things shift? Which of you suddenly changes behaviour? How?
- What happens after the shift? Do you both react differently to how you were acting at the beginning?
- What are the final payoffs? In what specific ways do you each feel bad? Do you opt to feel put down or do you put the other person down? Or do you both end up feeling down? Don't forget that feeling one-up is also negative.

Why is it happening?

Once you've understood the dynamics (and the existence) of a game, you can increase your awareness of how it comes about:

- Check out any tendencies you may have to act like a Victim, Rescuer or Persecutor. Use the Potency Pyramid in Figure 5.4 (see page 93). Recognize that it is okay for you and others to display vulnerability and ask for support, to behave in powerful ways when others genuinely need help, and to accept your share of responsibility for dealing with events.
- Check out your stroking pattern (see later in this chapter) – how can you get more positive strokes so you won't need the negative reinforcement from game playing?

- Consider the stroking pattern of your supervision partner – might you need to give them more positive strokes generally?

How can I change?

Once you've analysed what happens, worked out the dynamics and understood the underlying motivations, you're ready to move out of the game. It can be hard to do this while in the midst of it. Instead, use the prompts above to become aware and then consider what you might do differently, *before* the game even starts, to ensure a more constructive outcome.

Stephanie
Stephanie used to take taped segments of her work with clients to supervision but would consistently admit she had not yet analysed what was happening. The supervisor was a helpful sort and didn't like to criticize so he kept on providing detailed prompts while Stephanie slowly analysed. Stephanie continued to bring unanalysed tapes and he continued to help her.

The supervisor began to feel more and more frustrated but avoided saying so as he felt this was his own issue. Stephanie continued to plead lack of confidence in her ability to analyse without active prompting from the supervisor. The more impatient the supervisor felt, the more Stephanie retreated into acting like a helpless child.

The supervisor eventually lost patience and told Stephanie it was unlikely she would ever become a skilled coach if she was unwilling even to try analysing her work. At this point, Stephanie said she was shocked as the supervisor had not made it clear before how important this analysis was; she also complained that it was the fault of the supervisor for not teaching her properly. The session ended with both Stephanie and the supervisor feeling bad.

In his own supervision, the supervisor identified that the interactions with Stephanie could fit the pattern of a psychological game. He therefore identified options for responding differently before the game could get under way. This involved commencing a session, before any tapes could be produced, by explaining how prior analysis was not just about saving time in the supervision session; it was also a process whereby Stephanie would be building invaluable skills. Once she could do this readily, it would be a small step into analysing while she was working with the client, giving her many immediate options rather than having to take the client back over old ground after identifying better options in a supervision session.

He then introduced a staged process that involved Stephanie listening for specific things on her tapes (e.g. client questions) rather than analysing the whole thing. When she returned with an 'analysis' of the specifics, he made sure he praised her for completing this task. Gradually, he was able to have Stephanie add more specifics until, almost without realizing it, she was analysing fully.

Stroking patterns

In Chapter 5, I introduced the TA concept of strokes. Stroke is TA terminology for a unit of recognition. Strokes are anything that we (and other sentient beings) do to indicate to others that we are aware of their existence. Catching someone's eye, speaking to them, touching them are all strokes at different levels of intensity. Strokes are a biological necessity – children raised without strokes do not develop normally.

Positive strokes are those that invite a belief that self and others are okay; negative invite a sense of not-okayness about self, others or everyone (as in *I'm OK, You're OK* by Thomas Harris (1969) plus the variants of I'm OK, You're Not OK, I'm not and you are, or both of us are not). Negative strokes are better than being ignored; this is why society keeps solitary confinement as a serious punishment.

The strokes involved in supervision are extremely intense. To benefit from the supervision, the supervisee needs to be very open; in return, the supervisor gives their full attention. There are not many other relationships where the connection is so potent.

Such intensity comes with some risks. In the same way that clients may react to coaches as sources of strokes that are otherwise missing in their lives, and coaches may come to depend on their clients for strokes, so too may supervisees and supervisors fall into this trap, especially when they lack adequate stroking patterns generally.

When supervisees are too dependent on strokes from their supervisors, they are likely to choose client interventions based more on a supervisor's likely reaction than the needs of the client. Such supervisees may omit from supervision any work where they think the supervisor will not approve and instead select for supervision only those interventions they think the supervisor will like. They may become very upset if the supervisor gives constructive criticism, resent other supervisees and perceive the supervisor as a parent figure. This may lead then to want to spend as much time in supervision as possible so they may stretch things out or bring work that does not really need attention, and flatter the supervisor and generally aim to become a 'favourite'. These reactions are, of course, out of awareness.

When supervisors are too dependent on supervisees for strokes, they are likely to notice only those aspects of supervisees' interventions that they approve of, and avoid giving any negative feedback lest supervisees think they are nasty. Such supervisors may want to spend extra time with supervisees, letting sessions run over. They may also take on the characteristics of being a parent figure to particular supervisees, favouring them over other supervisees. Again, this will happen out of awareness, although other supervisees may of course notice what is happening.

Activity 8.2   Checking your stroking patterns

Review your stroking patterns for up to five professional and five personal contacts. Check whether you have adequate stroke supplies. Is there any possibility you could be using a supervision relationship to make up for any stroke deficit?

To check this out, draw up a chart in which you list the names of contacts in columns across the page and fill in comments under each name. You will then be able to spot any patterns.

Who are my key professional contacts?					
What strokes do I typically *give* each of them?					
Does this show healthy variety or am I treating everyone the same?					
What proportion of total strokes given by me is positive versus negative?					
Do I need to act to increase positives and decrease negatives?					
What strokes do I typically *get* from my professional contacts?					
Are these strokes that I value or are my contacts simply giving me their own preferred strokes?					
What proportion of total strokes being given to me is positive versus negative?					
Do I need to take action to change these proportions?					
Who are my key friends and/or family?					
What strokes do I typically *give* each of them?					
What strokes do I typically *get* from each of them?					
What proportion is positive versus negative?					

Do these proportions need to be changed?					
Do my professional and personal contacts combined provide me with enough positive strokes?					
Is there any chance I might be making up a deficit via my supervisor(s)?					
How can I make changes so that I am not reliant on my supervisor for strokes and can accept them as related to my professional development?					

Change and the competence curve

Reflection and supervision are processes that are intended to stimulate increased self-awareness; hence learning takes place and this leads to change. An understanding of change processes will enable us to maximize the opportunities for growth and minimize any potential distress.

A model based on death and grieving is often used to explain change processes. I think this is a very unhelpful metaphor because it implies that there must be pain and loss involved. I prefer to use a framework based on child development, so that there is a sense of curiosity and excitement about change.

I have taken a theory developed by Levin (1974) that describes the developmental tasks that children need to complete at various ages (see Hay 1996, for more details). We all fail to achieve these in some ways, even with the best of parenting. However, the positive message in Levin's work is that we recycle so we get several more opportunities to put things right. Levin also points out that we complete mini-cycles of the same sequence of stages after each of our own change points. Hence, we move house and it is rather like the process of being born and growing up, except not spread over so many years. Or we decide to become a coach and run the sequence as we develop into a professional.

I have added to this framework by linking the stages to what happens to our level of competence, which rises and falls depending on the stage we have reached. This gives us a **competence curve** as in Figure 8.1, showing how our performance is affected as we move through the stages.

The competence curve shows that as we enter into a change, our competence drops as we stop performing, then rises again as we act as if no change has occurred, then dips again as we struggle with realizing that our previous

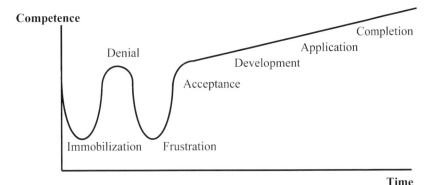

Figure 8.1 Competence curve
Source: Hay (1996)
Note: Not to scale

behaviour is no longer relevant, then rises and continues to rise as we adjust to the changed circumstances, start picking up the new skills we need, begin applying them and finally reach the point where we are no longer conscious of having been through a change.

This curve will apply to any changes, varying in the length of time taken depending on how significant the change has been for us. In childhood, it runs until we are 19 years old; it repeats on 19-year cycles. For a move into a management or professional role, it may take around two or three years to run. Moving to another desk may take only a few hours.

> *Vaz*
> When Vaz moved from business adviser to life coach, it took about two years for the cycle to run. At the beginning, he was somewhat dazed, although delighted, when told that he had been accepted into a coaching consultancy. Once he got into the work, he found that he was behaving as if he were still an expert business adviser instead of using a facilitative approach. As he realized this, he began to feel frustrated because there was so much to learn. He even castigated himself for taking the role and not realizing how different it would be. Fortunately, he moved beyond the frustration and was able to start thinking of himself as a life coaching professional. That made it easier for him to identify his own training needs and he was able to link up with an experienced life coach who was willing to pass on the benefits of experience. The consultancy company also arranged for some more formal training (plus supervision of course) at this stage. The more Vaz applied what he was learning, the less he felt like a newcomer. Eventually, about two years later, he realized that he now perceived himself as a life coach, albeit one who was committed to lifelong learning.

It is not always easy to run through the competence curve in the ideal way. Well-meaning colleagues and organizations will often interfere. Colleagues or managers may reassure us at the start of the change process, when we are least able to listen (this is why you need to put the facts in writing when you tell someone they are redundant – they don't hear what you say as this stage and need to be able to read it later on). Or they may attempt to provide training – again, a problem because until we've taken on the 'identity' of the new role, we're not clear about what we need to learn or why.

Another common organizationally-induced problem is that of another change being imposed before we've dealt with the last one. Perhaps we get as far as accepting that the change has occurred and being ready to learn new skills, and then we are told our job has changed again. We are plunged back into the immobilization, denial, frustration sequence again – and fail to get through to the positive feelings that go with the rest of the curve. No wonder organizations conclude that people resist change – this is a natural response if you are constantly denied the positive culmination of events.

Activity 8.3 Where are you on the competence curve?

Think back to the time when you first decided that you were going to become a coach. Answer the following questions until you reach the stage you are at now. Use your notes to reflect on how you might make future change processes as effective as possible.

	What went on for you during this period?	What helped? What hindered?
Recall your reaction when you first realized that you were going to become a coach. How long was it before you stopped floating on air or finding it hard to believe?		
How much time did you then spend doing what you'd done before, until you accepted that this was irrelevant to your new role?		
For how long did you struggle with feelings of frustration or anger about the new role, about not being able to perform instantly in the way you expected?		
How much time did you take to come to terms with your new identity?		

What training, coaching or other developmental activities did you engage in? Over what period of time?		
How did you apply what you were learning? What was the timeframe for you to work with clients to build up your skills?		
What told you that your change process was completed? When did you become aware that you now perceived yourself as a professional coach?		

You can of course use similar questions to reflect on supervision, plus:

When did you first decide to have supervision? Why?	
How did you behave at first?	
What happened as you became a coach who has regular supervision?	
How have you learned and then applied the skills of being a supervisee?	

Cycles of development

The competence curve will have an impact on what happens during supervision. Understanding the model can help us work out why some stages of supervision seem to run better than others. This will allow supervisor and/or supervisee to initiate activities that will contribute to a more effective experience.

To understand the process more deeply, it usually helps to know something about Levin's original work. She identified several stages during childhood, the **cycles of development**, along with the developmental tasks that the child needs to complete, and what is involved in parenting so that this is possible. Figure 8.2 provides a summary of these, showing how problems at different ages may affect us in later life; and how, because we also have repeated opportunities to revisit unfinished developmental tasks, a supervisor can respond in ways that will best match the needs of the supervisee.

Developmental task	Problems if not yet attained	What we need from a supervisor
Being 0–6 months – relates to Immobilization		
We are supposed to simply 'be'. We need people around us who demonstrate their love and affection – and who do not expect us to do anything more than be a baby.	We feel at a deep level that we have no right to exist. We may simply freeze, as if waiting for someone else to do something.	That they are genuinely pleased we are there, that they do not seem to have any particular expectations of us, we can be ourselves and relax in their presence.
Exploring 6–18 months – relates to Denial		
We explore the world. We touch, suck, grasp, become mobile. We need the adults to encourage our natural curiosity while ensuring a safe structure – no knives or naked flames within our reach.	We may be afraid to explore the world – or we may act in a counter-phobic manner and engage in dangerous activities. We may be very reluctant to reflect on or analyse our behaviour.	That they provide an environment that feels safe to explore within – that the supervisor will make sure we do not harm ourselves, and that no-one else can harm us. We can make mistakes and learn rather than being punished.
Thinking 1½–2 years – relates to Frustration		
We learn to think for ourselves. We may seem to be challenging but in reality we are using our own thinking skills to make decisions while lacking access to the information the grown-ups are using.	We don't learn to think, we associate expressing our own thoughts with negative consequences, we expect others to make decisions on our behalf and to just tell us what to do.	That they are patient, avoid telling us what to do, keep prompting us to think for ourself. We can express opinions and challenge authority without getting into trouble.
Identity 3–6 years – relates to Acceptance		
We make some significant decisions about our identity. We decide what sort of person we are – perhaps a tomboy female, a macho male, or someone just like a favourite relative.	We adopt an identity that is not really us, we believe we have characteristics that have been attributed to us by others, that our life will follow some pre-set script, we are not autonomous about who we really are.	That they challenge us to make our own decisions about our identity, they avoid reinforcing unhelpful self-beliefs, they treat us as an autonomous decision-maker.

Developmental task	Problems if not yet attained	What we need from a supervisor
Skills 6–12 years – relates to Development		
We set out to acquire the skills that will fit our identity and enable us to function in the world. In other words, we learn how to be adults – with varying degrees of success depending on who our role models and teachers are!	We are at the mercy of our role models so there may be things we just don't know how to do, or ways of behaving we've copied that are unacceptable. We may also lack experiences of having learned skills successfully.	That they are a good enough role model and/or can refer us to others who can help us acquire skills Conversely, that they avoid any tendency to turn us into a clone of them.
Integration 12–18 years – relates to Application		
We are 'pulling our personality together'! In fact, we recycle the earlier stages. Thus, 13-year-olds often act like babies and toddlers, to the despair of the adults around them. We may rethink our identity, perhaps having found a new role model, and then we acquire even more life skills. We (hopefully) finally emerge as an adult and promptly start the process again.	Any of the problems we have from deficits at earlier stages may be reinforced during this stage. We may fail to integrate the various aspects, particularly if we have significant developmental needs still unmet.	That they provide responses appropriate to whichever earlier stage is impacting now. That they treat us as grown-ups (or at least as teenagers) rather than as a child, they make it clear we are capable of sorting out our own lives, that we can seek out more information about the world, and that in the end they are there as professional colleagues rather than parent figures.

Figure 8.2 Summary of developmental tasks

Activity 8.4 Where are you within the cycles of development?

Levin has established that the 18-year pattern of the cycles can be tracked by dividing your age by 19 (i.e. to end of eighteenth year) and the remainder will be where you are in your current cycle. It seems also that dividing by 13 years and taking the remainder will also have significance. In addition, if you are bringing up children, you are likely to parallel the stages of each child, overlaid with your own pattern.

So check this out and see where you are in the overall spiral. 19 and 13 may or may not give you the same remainder – there may be two stages vying for priority in your life right now.

Keep in mind that this is your time for re-cycling so you have the opportunity to re-work any stages where the previous outcome was unsatisfactory.

Check out the following prompts for the age within the cycle that you have reached:

- How well have you been able in the past to meet your developmental needs for this stage? Are you still struggling from previous deficits? Or are you re-experiencing a stage where things go well for you?
- How might previous deficits (and satisfactory development) be influencing your life now? What might you still be seeking?
- How might you 'organize' your life so that your developmental needs will be met?
- What impact might these needs be having on your reflection and/or supervision processes? What can you do to ensure that your needs do not interfere with these processes?
- What might you need to share with your reflection colleagues and/or supervisor so that they can provide the most appropriate support and challenge to you?

Working styles

There are various models that allow us to identify our styles of behaviour or personality: over the years I've administered Myers-Briggs Type Indicator® (see OPP at www.opp.eu.com/), Learning Styles Questionnaire (Honey and Mumford 1986), Enneagram RHETI (Riso and Hudson 2003 see www.enneagraminstitute.com/), Kirton Innovation-Adaptation Inventory (Kirton 1999), Cattell's 16PF (see OPP at www.opp.cu.com/) – and there are many more as a quick search on the internet will show.

If you are familiar with any such models, they can be useful for analysing your reflection patterns and supervisory relationships. It helps if you and your supervisor are familiar with the same model, so that you have a shared map of the world to use. However, even if you can't find a common model, you can always use my favourite, working styles, because it is simple and takes little time to understand and start applying.

The working styles model (Hay 1996) is based on the concept of 'drivers' (Kahler 1979). Drivers in this case refer to five characteristic ways in which people respond to stress, as captured in the labels for the styles: Hurry Up, Be Perfect, Please People, Try Hard, and Be Strong. They are called drivers because they take over and *drive* us, so that the more stressed we become, the more of the characteristic style we exhibit, even though by then it is usually making things worse. I label it working style when we have it under conscious control, when it is usually seen as our strength, and reserve the original term of driver for those times when we believe we have no choice about our behaviour.

All of us have a little of all of the styles, of course, but most of us will recognize that one or two styles predominate. Thus Hurry Ups get lots done, Be Perfects are great on detail, Please People are caring, Try Hards are enthusiastic and Be Strongs are calm in a crisis. Put us under too much stress, though, and the driver kicks in and Hurry Ups get increasingly impatient and make mistakes, Be Perfects become pedantic, critical and obsessive about checking, Please People get paranoid about upsetting anyone, Try Hards keep starting new things and finishing none of them, and Be Strongs go into robot mode, refuse any help and behave insensitively.

Hurry Up

Hurry Ups want to do everything quickly. They talk fast, interrupt others, make quick decisions, and get lots done. This productivity may not be helpful with a client who needs to be listened to; it may also cause problems in supervision as the supervisee may get impatient and want to rush the process. Hurry Ups typically hate reflecting at any length – instead, they prefer to listen to an overview and quickly pick up on the most obvious areas for attention – and then can hardly wait to rush off and do some more client work.

Alternatively, Hurry Ups leave things until the last minute, although they do then respond well to impending deadlines. This means they prepare only in the few minutes before a client arrives, and they are likely to be reflecting just before the supervision session begins. They therefore have no spare time to do a bit more reflecting on any intriguing aspects – and they will emit signals that the supervisor should move on quickly too.

All this haste means that Hurry Ups often make mistakes and overlook significant aspects. They need others to spot the discounting and insist they slow down and reflect more thoroughly. If the supervisor is also a Hurry Up, the two together are likely to work very quickly and very superficially – and to feel very comfortable with each other.

Another common problem for Hurry Ups is that they are polyphonic – they tend to be juggling lots of tasks at once (the 'take a book, a sandwich and a mobile phone to the toilet' syndrome). To a Hurry Up, spending time reflecting on something that has already been done may seem a waste of time. Supervisors may need to challenge them to take time out to develop increased competence.

Be Perfect

This style is in some ways the opposite of Hurry Up, making for interesting dynamics when the two styles are working together. Be Perfects aim to be just that – perfect – which is of course something that is reserved for Allah and not for mortals. Be Perfects are therefore usually fairly accurate because they check everything, and well organized because they plan ahead and build in contingencies so they will do a perfect job.

Unfortunately, all this checking takes time so Be Perfects often miss deadlines. Their taped work will not have been analysed thoroughly enough to play it to anyone else, or they are spending so long writing up notes that they have insufficient time left to reflect properly.

Paired with another Be Perfect may mean that supervision becomes an extremely thorough reflection, over several sessions, but always on the same piece of work so it will be reviewed 'perfectly'. Paired with a Hurry Up may be very helpful in challenging behaviour patterns but may also lead to outright war.

A particular difficulty for Be Perfects is that they often struggle to accept feedback. When you have a map of the world that requires you to Be Perfect, it can challenge your very being when you are told that you could improve on what you've done. Be Perfect supervisees may need extra support to get over their own unrealistic expectations of themselves.

Please People

People with this working style are very nice to have around. They are intuitive and caring. However, when the driver takes over, they become increasingly anxious about offending anyone, they attempt to mind-read and do things to please others, and then feel hurt when their efforts are not appreciated. Sometimes, they may switch to a parent mode and expect others to please them.

When reflecting, Please People may be too ready to conclude that they have let the client down. They may fail to challenge a client in case they upset them, and then feel bad afterwards for not challenging. They may also feel the client has let them down if the client fails to behave in the way the coach thinks they should (and was perhaps trying to hint at). They may spend a lot of time worrying about whether they are helpful enough to clients generally.

In supervision, this pattern may mean that the supervisees take any feedback personally. If you believe you should be pleasing others, then you must also please your supervisors – if they appear to think you could have done better, then you have failed. Please People supervisees may also want to tell supervisors only about those aspects of their work, or clients, that they believe supervisors will like.

Conversely, Please People supervisors may find it hard to give any constructive criticism for fear of hurting supervisees' feelings. They may avoid certain areas and focus only on 'safe' aspects where they can compliment the supervisees. This may feel very supportive but may mean that the supervisees take longer to recognize where they need to change.

Try Hard

If at first you don't succeed, try, try again. This style results in people who put a lot of effort and enthusiasm into whatever they are doing, but who may not see things through to successful completion. In coaching, they may be innovative in how they work with clients but may then spoil this by trying out too many ideas without following any of them up properly.

Try Hard supervisees may be inclined to pick up several possibilities and find it difficult to choose one when they are next with a client. They may be like a 'fashion victim', enthusiastically trying out every new approach or technique they learn – and failing to practise any of them consistently enough to develop competence. Try Hard supervisors may repeat this pattern with supervisees. And put the two together and you may have a recipe for much enthusiasm but little sustained implementation.

Another particularly difficult combination is Try Hard with Be Perfect – the Be Perfect may react very badly to someone who seems to start things and not finish them while the Try Hard struggles to stay enthusiastic through a mass of detail. During supervision sessions, it may seem as if the Try Hard goes off on tangents all the time, while the Be Perfect plods through a paralysis by analysis procedure.

Be Strong

The strengths of the Be Strong include calmness, especially in a crisis, plus conscientiousness – no ducking the unpleasant tasks. The weaknesses when the style is overdone tend to be insensitivity, refusal to do anything other than work steadily through tasks as they come up (no changing priorities, no extra effort), and a failure to ask for help when they can't cope.

The calmness can be a definite asset to coaches, especially with clients who bring 'shock' revelations. The conscientiousness is also useful as Be Strong coaches will work with clients that others might find distasteful. However, the potential drawback is that coaches may then fail to recognize issues that need to be brought to supervision. They may instead present as if everything is straightforward and overlook significant emotional processes.

The Be Strong belief that one must manage alone may also interfere with supervision. There may be a tendency to stay silent about the more difficult clients, and to struggle to cope with problems for which supervisees lack adequate experience. Supervisors may need a high level of skill at probing to find out what is really going on – and even then, supervisees may find it difficult to accept support.

Be Strong supervisors may inadvertently give the impression that asking for help is a sign of weakness. And put two Be Strongs together and supervision is likely to focus only on practicalities, as if emotions do not exist.

Activity 8.5   Identify your working style(s)

Use the prompts below to become more aware of your characteristic working style or styles. For each style, there are a couple of potential strengths that may be exhibited and a couple of unhelpful behaviours. Tick those that are like you and make notes on how they show up.

Working style	√	How I behave in this style
Hurry Up		
works quickly, responds well to deadlines		
gets a lot done in a short time		
makes mistakes, lacks attention to detail		
gets impatient, finishes others' sentences		
Be Perfect		
is accurate, checks carefully		
well organized, looks ahead for potential problems		
includes too much detail, checks over and over		
criticizes over minor details, rarely satisfied		
Please People		
good team member, encourages harmony		
intuitive and aware, considers others		
anxious for approval of others, will not confront		
feels misunderstood, hurt by criticism		
Try Hard		
enthusiastic, energetic with new ideas		
thorough at following up all possibilities		
loses interest and moves on to new things		
tends not to finish, others have to take over		
Be Strong		
calm under pressure, copes with stress		
conscientious, strong sense of duty		
will not ask for help or admit weakness		
may seem cold and distant, or overly jovial		

Activity 8.6   Working styles in supervision

Produce a chart using the following headings to review the impact of your working style(s) on how you approach reflection, and of how your style and that of your supervisor may combine within the supervisory relationship.

Note which working style(s) you believe is/are most characteristic of you.		
What positive indicators of these do you notice in your practice?		
What negative indicators appear sometimes?		
What effect does each style have on how you reflect on your work?		
What effect does each style have on your approach to supervision?		
How might you change your approach to get more benefit from supervision?		
Which working style(s) do you believe are most characteristic of your supervisor?		
What positive indicators of your supervisor's working style(s) do you notice during supervision?		
How does your supervisor's working style(s) interact positively with yours?		
What negative indicators of your supervisor's working style(s) appear sometimes?		
How does your supervisor's working style(s) interact negatively with yours?		
Taking into account the mix of your own and your supervisor's working styles, how might you change your approach to get more benefit from supervision?		
Do you need to discuss this with your supervisor?		

9 Cross-cultural Considerations

Before you read on I suggest that you use Activity 9.1 to reflect on your current experiences and fantasies around working with difference. After that, this chapter will invite you to review your contracting; I will then summarize some key elements of cultural differences and invite you to consider how these might apply in your practice. Finally, I include some material and activities related to coaching schemes and to organizational contexts.

Activity 9.1   Fantasies and fears

Use the headings below to prompt you to think about a range of 'difference' factors. There are no right or wrong answers; this is an awareness-raising activity.

In respect of:	Your experiences of working with 'difference' and with 'similarity'	Possible advantages and drawbacks within a mentoring relationship
sex		
age group		
cultural background		
ethnic origin		
race		
colour		
religious background		
sexual orientation		
physical disability		
educational experiences		
professional background		
any other form of diversity		

Cross-cultural contracting

Chapter 7 contained detailed material on three levels of contracting: procedural, professional and psychological. I will give a brief recap and highlight the potential cross-cultural implications.

The *procedural* level refers to the administrative aspects of coaching, such as how often and for how long you will meet, who will make the necessary arrangements, what documentation is required, etc. There may be significant cultural norms about who initiates appointments, the importance (or otherwise) of timekeeping, and the reactions to any cancellations. There may also be different responses to the use of documentation, with some seeing it simply as an administrative chore while others may be virtually paranoid about how it will be used (having had bad experiences with bureaucrats or others in the past).

The *professional* level relates to the format and intended outcome of the coaching, such as whether the coach is a sponsor or not, whether expert teaching or coaching is involved, what other relationships might be involved – or often, what will not be involved, such as the coach intervening on behalf of the client at the place of work. Again, there may be significantly different expectations. Coaching approaches vary across cultures – some focus on individual growth, others emphasize the need for teamwork, others have strong elements of role modelling and traditional mentoring roles, and yet others have a sports coaching flavour.

The *psychological* level is a highly significant level as it refers to elements of the coaching relationship that are often out of awareness. There may be issues related to client dependency or resentment, or unspoken, and maybe unconscious, concerns about diversity and difference. The quality of most relationships, of any kind, is determined at the unconscious, psychological level.

We can add two more levels when practising cross-culturally: perceptual and political. The *perceptual* level refers to the ways the relationship is viewed, some of which may also be at the psychological level. There may be a perception (by coach, client or 'onlookers') that coaching is about sponsors and protégés; there may be cynicism from others who do not have a place on the scheme; there may even be suspicions about mixed sex or mixed race pairings.

The *political* level is about the impact of the context. We cannot avoid being within a socio-political framework. We need to take into account factors such as the ways in which power operates; for instance, are we working to inculturate minority groups into the dominant culture (knowingly or unknowingly), are we attempting to create a mixed culture, or are we aiming to maintain separate, co-existing cultures?

Activity 9.2   Cross-cultural contracting

Use the following questions to prompt you in reviewing the different levels of contracting. You might also want to return to this list occasionally – it is not realistic to think that you will answer every question the first time you do this. Instead, allow yourselves to return to the questions as you build your relationship.

As with a legal contract, you can always make changes to your contract. Starting with an explicit contract makes it easier to know what you want to change, and simpler to discuss and agree those changes.

Procedural

- Who is responsible for arranging meetings?
- How often and for how long should each meeting last?
- Where shall we meet?
- Who takes responsibility for ensuring our meetings are private and uninterrupted?
- What arrangements shall we have for cancellations?
- What documentation is required – by us or the organization (or institution e.g. a learning log, evidence of continuous professional development, notes for a portfolio, etc.)?
- Who will complete the documentation and where will it be kept?

Professional

- What is the purpose of the coaching?
- How does it fit with the rest of our professional lives?
- What do we expect to gain from being in a coaching relationship?
- What knowledge, skills, experience does the coach bring to the relationship?
- What knowledge, skills, experience does the client bring to the relationship?
- What skills, knowledge, experience and expertise might be acquired from elsewhere?
- What support does the organization provide (e.g. practical support, training)?
- How will we take back our learning into our respective workplaces and/or lives?

Psychological

- How do we each really feel about the relationship?
- How will we be honest with each other in respectful ways?
- How can we raise our level of mutual awareness and understanding of each other?
- What 'secret' fears do we have, especially about our differences?
- How will we deal with any misunderstandings, including those we think may be due to cultural differences?

- What might go wrong? What plans do we have for dealing with problems?
- How will we bring the relationship to a healthy end when the time comes?
- How will we end the relationship at any time if either of us feels it is not working (i.e. what arrangements shall we have for a *no fault divorce*)?

Perceptual

- What are our perceptions of each other?
- How much are these perceptions influenced by our differences?
- How much are these perceptions influenced by our similarities?
- How might others perceive each of us?
- What might others think of our relationship and arrangements?
- What misunderstandings might others have?
- What factors might influence the perceptions of others, e.g. appearance, behaviour?
- How can we best manage other people's perceptions?

Political

- What awareness do we each have about racism, sexism, etc. in society in general and how this affects people at work?
- What experiences have either of us had about racism, sexism, etc. at work and what happened?
- What is the culture of our organization(s) and how might this affect the outcomes of our relationship?
- How will we avoid the trap of operating only within the dominant cultural paradigm?
- How might others be affected by cultural paradigms and what might we need to do to counter the effects of that?
- How will we balance the individual needs of the client with the urge to change society?
- How will we support each other in learning to think outside our existing cultural frames of reference?

Some stereotypes

The following ideas are based on analyses by various people of the major differences between cultures.

Individual or group

Many cultures, especially in the West, tend to believe that individual motivation is paramount; in the East, however, the group is generally regarded as far more important. This means that people in the USA, for instance, will pay a lot of attention to individual performance, individual motivation, individual reward systems. In Asia, on the other hand, they are much more likely to focus on team performance, ways to have the team work well together, and team rewards.

In an individualist culture, people want to excel and may even withhold information or support because they believe they are in competition with their colleagues for promotion or recognition. In group cultures, people do not want to be singled out and may go along with group decisions instead of speaking out when the group is wrong.

Rules or relationships

In some cultures there is great emphasis on following the rules. In other cultures, rules come second to relationships – if a friend needs help, you break the rules.

If you apply this thinking to something related to work, the questions suggested in Activity 9.2 might be extended to include what would you do if you find out that a friend is cheating on their expense claims? (A rules person would report them; a relationships person would not.) And would your decision change if the friend were embezzling large sums – or needed the money to pay for an operation for a sick child?

The main difference here is that some people will believe that the rules should be applied totally, to everyone. Others will believe that we should always take the person's situation into account. Such different points of view can lead to major misunderstandings.

Facts or feelings

Some people make decisions based on logic; others take into account how people will feel. Those who value logic will want the facts and are likely to start doing business without needing much time to build a relationship. Those who take feelings into account will want to get to know someone really well before they are prepared to talk business.

At a general business level, this may show up as opposing views about the importance of costs and/or profits versus being an organization that cares for its employees. Decisions based on logic will focus on income and expenditure, share prices, and so on, and may lead to redundancies when times are bad; decisions based on feelings will concentrate on maintaining jobs even though money is tight and may of course make the financial situation worse.

Those who take the feelings approach will argue that they are keeping valuable skills within the organization for the future when the situation improves; those who make the logical decisions will be more likely to claim that there will be no organization if the financial losses are too substantial. The truth may be somewhere in between.

Emotion

In some cultures people show their emotions readily; in others, people seem much more controlled and neutral. Neither is better – they are simply different. However, such a difference can lead to much discomfort. Those who show little emotion may feel overwhelmed by displays of feelings, or may believe that emotional people are somehow unbalanced. Those who display their emotions may start to believe that those with less overt feelings are cold and unfriendly, or that they are refusing to behave like normal human beings.

Control

Within some cultures people act as if they can control the world; in others, people expect to live in harmony with their environment. Some people attribute events to their own actions; others believe that fate is the deciding factor. Such differences may show up as a commitment to increased advertising to generate more sales during a recession versus an acceptance of the need to cut back until the market improves.

Status

Within some areas of the world, people gain status by being successful, getting promoted, achieving results and being rewarded for this. In other parts of the world, status is measured by the position that someone holds, so the status comes first and then the person is expected to achieve results that match their position.

This may have considerable impact within an organization. It will affect whether people are promoted from within because they have done a good job, or whether they are brought in from outside and expected to succeed because they are appointed to a position with status built into it.

Time

Finally, one major distinction between cultures – how people view time. In many countries, particularly in the West, time is viewed as something to be controlled. It is also regarded as sequential – one thing happens after another so you can put dates and times in your diary to represent what you plan to do.

In other parts of the world, particularly the East and South America, time is something that flows by while you do things. What you are doing is more important than the time at which you do it. You start whenever you are ready to start and you finish whenever the activity is complete.

The different ways we view time is one of the major problems across cultures. Those on sequential time expect to make appointments, keep them, do what needs to be done, and move onto the next appointment at the correct time. Those on synchronic time expect to synchronize whatever needs to happen, so they interrupt appointments to talk to someone else, do several things at once, start meetings late or not at all, and respond happily to interruptions.

Activity 9.3   Reflecting on stereotypes

Use the chart below to identify some examples of coaching situations where diversity could have (or did) lead to conflict or collusion. Make brief notes about each viewpoint. Plan how more useful outcomes might be achieved.

Identify			
Type of diversity	Coach viewpoint	Client viewpoint	What I might do in future
Individual or Group			
Rules or Relationships			
Facts or Feelings			
Emotion			
Control			
Status			
Time			
Add your own examples here			

Cross-cultural schemes

In response to a question from me about cultural awareness training for mentors on a scheme for refugees in a European country, the scheme co-ordinator told me that this was unnecessary because 'the mentees are required to adopt the norms of this country now'. There was no apparent awareness of how the distress of being a refugee might be compounded by culturally insensitive mentors. Instead the implications were that mentors already knew all they could possibly need to know; that the cultural norms of the refugees were unimportant and irrelevant; that refugees could somehow acquire new cultural norms without mentors needing to be trained to help them with this, and a boundary was set against any possibilities that the existing cultural norms might be enhanced by the addition of norms brought by the refugees or that mentors might also learn from their mentees.

This is probably an extreme example but I use it because it illustrates how easy it is to become locked inside our own frame of reference. The co-ordinator was running a socially responsible scheme, designed by the national government to help the refugees become assimilated into their new country. The mentors were volunteers who wanted to welcome the refugees. Everyone involved had the best of intentions; everyone was also discounting the very existence of the maps of the world belonging to the unfortunate refugees.

We can use a variation of the steps to success model described in Chapter 3 to reflect on national or organizational factors.

Activity 9.4   Steps to cross-cultural success

Situation

- How do people behave?
- What are the proportions of people from different sexes and from different ethnic backgrounds?
- How many hold which jobs at what levels?
- What is the spread of qualifications across groups?

Significance

- What examples have there been of sexist or racist behaviour?
- How do these relate statistically to total numbers of people?
- How well do the proportions of people working at different levels, etc. match the available pools of people?
- What discrimination might be in operation relating to the clients?

Solutions

- What policies exist to ensure equality?
- What procedures exist to ensure equality?
- What changes are needed to ensure greater equality?
- What can be done about any discrimination or perceived discrimination?

Skills

- What levels of skills are there within the organization (or country) for cross-cultural communications and working?
- Who has the skills to bring about any necessary changes?

- What skills do the clients have for working cross-culturally?
- How might the clients acquire additional skills?
- What skills do the coaches have for working cross-culturally?
- How might the coaches acquire additional skills?

Strategies

- How are policies and practices being implemented to minimize discrimination and increase diversity?
- What can be done to ensure a balance between cultures?
- How best can the clients develop appropriate cross-culturalism without losing their identity?
- Who else might be involved in developing genuine cross-culturalism?
- How best can the organization (or nation) benefit from cross-culturalism?

Success

- What might the clients gain by changing their own cultural perceptions?
- What might the clients lose by changing their own cultural perceptions?
- What ongoing support exists for the clients?
- Who are the champions of diversity?
- What might the coaches gain by changing their own cultural perceptions?
- What might the coaches lose by changing their own cultural perceptions?
- What ongoing support exists for the coaches?

What Now?

Having read this far, you may well be wondering 'What now?' – or you may be feeling somewhat overloaded by the range of theories and activities. 'What now' may, therefore, need to be some form of prioritization.

I have mentioned several times throughout this book that its content is there for you to select what you need. There is no intention that you work through everything, or that you do so in the order that things appear in the book. You can focus on whatever aspects seem most relevant at the time and you can always come back to the rest later.

To establish a basis for your choices of where to start, you could, for example, use the notion of an action planning tree (described in Chapter 5, see Figure 5.7, page 96) to map out your own action plan in terms of becoming an increasingly competent professional coach.

That leaves us with the longer term. One of the things that 'good' supervisors do is pay attention to the developmental direction of each supervisee. Supervision is about the meta perspective of the supervisees' practices but there is also the still wider view of the supervisees' professional careers – or even the need sometimes to help supervisees recognize they might want a different professional role.

So, as my final set of prompts, here are some to help you reflect on your medium-term and long-term actions:

- Using any scale you like (1 to 5, low–medium–high, etc.), rate your current level of competence, your intended level in two years time, and the level you ultimately intend to reach.
- Draw together your responses to the various activities in this book, and incorporate any other sources of information about your practice, and write a 'school report' about yourself that highlights your strengths and development needs.
- Think about your professional identity – are you a professional coach or is the coaching done alongside another role (e.g. manager, consultant, supervisor)? What implications does this have for your ongoing development?
- Consider your timescale – how many years to reach what you regard as fully competent? How long before you might make a career change? Is retirement on the horizon?

And as a final activity, sketch out a timeline into the future and indicate your various priorities along it. Use this as your prompt to revisit various parts of this book – and, of course, to incorporate other elements with your ongoing development.

And as a final reflection, review your timeline with your supervisor and/ or your reflection colleagues.

Glossary

The entries in this glossary are shown in bold on their first occurrence in the text.

1st, 2nd, 3rd, 4th position – see perceptual position

80/20 principle – proposition that any characteristic of a large group will be distributed so that 20 per cent of the group 'own' 80 per cent of the characteristic; also known as Pareto principle

Adult – see *ego states*

auditory – see *representational systems*

Be Perfect – see *working styles*

Be Strong – see *working styles*

C5P5A5 – model for reflecting on the process of practice or the process of supervision

calibration – process of 'measuring' another person's reactions so we 'read' them

Child – see *ego states*

coach, coaching – not defined as there are so many variations, see coach/mentoring

coach/mentoring – term introduced by the EMCC to make the point that coaching and mentoring definitions so often overlap

competence curve – model for understanding the stages people go through after change

contract, contracting – agreement between stakeholders about the nature of their ongoing professional relationship

countertransference – unwittingly accepting someone else's transference onto you and responding as if you really are the person that others believe you to be

cycles of development – model of how children develop and how this recycles throughout adult life

dependent symbiosis – see symbiosis

discounting – unwitting process whereby we 'overlook' some aspect of ourself, others and/or the situation

drama triangle – model of Persecutor, Rescuer and Victim positions that are involved in *psychological games*

drivers – see *working styles*

dual relationships – relationships where we have more than one way of relating, e.g. as coach and as assessor to the same person

ego states – systems of thinking, feeling and behaving, typically observed as like a parent, child or adult

extraversion/introversion – see *MBTI*®

force field analysis – framework to aid decision-making by comparing forces for and against

games – see *psychological games*

Hurry Up – see *working styles*

I'm OK, You're OK, or not OK – see *windows on the world*

judging/perceiving – see *MBTI*®

kinaesthetic – see *representational systems*

language patterns – framework for classifying the patterns in how we speak, which also explains potential hypnotic impact of much of what we say

life positions – see *windows on the world*

M&Ms – goal-setting checklist – measurable, manageable, motivational

Martians and Venusians – metaphor for gender differences

MBTI® **(Myers-Briggs Type Inventory**®**)** – measure of psychological preferences

mentoring – see coach/mentoring

meta programs – software of the brain/mind, familiar ways individuals have of thinking, feeling and deciding

meta position – see perceptual position

Myers-Briggs – see *MBTI*®

neurological levels – levels at which change may occur, e.g. our environment, our beliefs

parallel process – phenomenon whereby people in one setting may duplicate (parallel) interactions by people in another setting

Parent – see *ego states*

Pareto – see 80/20 principle

perceptual position – a 'place' from which you can take a view, such as other person's shoes, unbiased observer, etc.

Persecutor – see drama triangle

Please People – see *working styles*

potency pyramid – model for avoiding negative positions on the *drama triangle*

pre-suppositions – the beliefs we must have in order for what we say to be true, e.g. 'What film shall we see?' implies pre-supposition that we are going to see a film together

psychological distance – the felt or fantasized distance between parties to a *contract*

psychological games – repetitive sequences of interactions that have hidden messages and lead to negative outcomes

R4C4P4 – set of ground rules for groups

rapport – phenomenon of being in close contact with another person

Rescuer – see drama triangle

reflective practice – reviewing your practice with a view to ongoing competence development

regression – what happens when we unwittingly revert to feeling, thinking and behaving as we did when we were younger; may also present as if we are a clone of someone who was around when we were younger

representational systems – ways we perceive and process what is going on; most commonly visual, auditory and kinaesthetic (VAK)

Rescuer – see drama triangle

self reflection – see reflective practice

sensing/intuitive – see *MBTI®*

situational anchors – items in the environment that act as triggers and re-stimulate specific reactions from the past

SPECTRE – checklist for comparing contextual influences: social, political, economic, competitive, technological, regulatory, environmental

stakeholders – those involved in any coaching or supervisory relationship, whether directly or indirectly

steps to success – model for overcoming *discounting*

strokes, stroking – any of our interactions may be viewed as units of recognition of another person's existence

supervision – process of helping a supervisee to take a super-vision, or meta perspective, of their practice or elements of it

symbiosis – phenomenon whereby two people behave as if they are only one person between them, e.g. one parents and the other acts as if a child

symbiosis, competitive – two people both seeking to be the parent or the child in the relationship

thinking/feeling – see *MBTI®*

transference – 'transferring' the characteristics, or even the entire person, of one person onto another; behaving unwittingly as if a person were someone else

Try Hard – see *working styles*

VAK – see *representational systems*

visual – see *representational systems*

windows on the world – model of ways in which we may distort our perceptions to reinforce our overall frame of reference

working styles – framework of five characteristic ways of behaving, which may also present as 'drivers' so we feel compelled to act in such a style

victim – see drama triangle

Bibliography

Bandler, Richard and Grinder, John (1975a) *Structure of Magic*, vol. I. Science and Behavior Books.

Bandler, Richard and Grinder, John (1975b) *Patterns of the Hypnotic Techniques of Milton H. Erickson M.D.* Meta Publications.

Berne, Eric (1961) *Transactional Analysis in Psychotherapy*. Grove Press.

Berne, Eric (1964) *Games People Play*. London: Penguin Books Ltd.

Cameron-Bandler, L., Gordon, D. and Lebeau, M. (1985) *The Emprint Method*. FuturePace Inc.

Campbell, Joseph (1973) *The Hero with a Thousand Faces*. Princeton, NJ: Princeton University Press.

Charvet, Shelley Rose (1997) *Words that Change Minds: Mastering the Language of Influence*. Kendall/Hunt Publishing.

Clarkson, Petruska (1991) *Transactional Analysis Psychotherapy*. London: Routledge.

Dilts, Robert (1990) *Changing Belief Systems with NLP*. Meta Publications.

Dilts, Robert (1994) *Strategies of Genius*, vol. I. Meta Publications.

English, Fanita (1975) The three cornered contract, *Transactional Analysis Journal*.

Gray, John (1993) *Men Are from Mars, Women Are from Venus*. London: Thorsons/ Harper Collins.

Grinder, John and Delozier, Judith (1995) *Turtles All the Way Down: Prerequisites for Personal Growth*. Metamorphous Press.

Harris, Thomas (1969) *I'm OK, You're OK*. Avon Books.

Hawkins, Peter and Shohet, Robin (2000) *Supervision in the Helping Professions*, 2nd edn. Maidenhead: Open University Press.

Hay, Julie (1993) *Working it Out at Work: Understanding Attitudes and Building Relationships*. Watford: Sherwood Publishing.

Hay, Julie (1995) *Donkey Bridges for Developmental TA: Making Transactional Analysis Memorable and Accessible*. Watford: Sherwood Publishing.

Hay, Julie (1996) *Transactional Analysis for Trainers*. Watford: Sherwood Publishing.

Hay, Julie (1998) *NLP Practitioner Training Handout Manual*. Watford: Sherwood Publishing.

Hay, Julie (1999) *Transformational Mentoring: Creating Developmental Alliances for Changing Organizational Cultures*. Watford: Sherwood Publishing.

Hay, Julie (2000) SPECTRE (and timelining), *INTAND Newsletter*, 8(3).

Honey, Peter and Mumford, Alan (1986) *The Manual of Learning Styles*. Peter Honey.

Kahler, Taibi (1979) *Process Therapy in Brief.* Human Development Publications.

Karpman, Stephen (1968) Fairy tales and script drama analysis, *Transactional Analysis Bulletin.*

Kelley, Robert E. (1985) *The Gold Collar Worker: Harnessing the Brain Power of the New Work Force.* Reading, MA: Addison-Wesley.

Kirton, Michael (1999) *Kirton Adaptation-Innovation Inventory (KAI) Manual,* 3rd edn. KAI Distribution Centre, UK (reprinted with amendments 2005).

Koch, Richard (1997) *80/20 Principle: The Secret of Achieving More with Less.* London: Nicholas Brealey.

Kolb, D.A. (1984) *Experiential Learning.* Englewood Cliffs, NJ: Prentice-Hall.

Lakoff, George and Johnson, Mark (1980) *Metaphors We Live By.* Chicago: University of Chicago Press.

Levin, Pamela (1974) *Becoming the Way We Are.* Health Communications Inc.

Lewin Kurt (1951) *Field Theory in Social Science.* New York: Harper and Row.

Mellor, Ken and Schiff, Eric (1975) Discounting, *Transactional Analysis Journal.*

Micholt, Nelly (1992) Psychological distance and group interventions, *Transactional Analysis Journal.*

Molden, David (1996) *Managing with the Power of NLP.* London: Pitman Publishing.

Novellino, Michele and Moiso, Carlo (1990) The psychodynamic approach to transactional analysis, *Transactional Analysis Journal,* 20(3): 187–92.

O'Connor, Joseph (1998) *Leading with NLP.* London: Thorsons.

Pareto, Vilfredo (1896/7) *Cours d'Economique Politique.* Lausanne: Lausanne University.

Proctor, Brigid (1986) 'Supervision: a co-operative exercise in accountability', in A. Marken and M. Payne (eds) *Enabling and Ensuring: Supervision in Practice.* Leicester: Leicester National Youth Bureau/Council for Education and Training in Youth and Community Work.

Riso, Don Richard and Hudson, Russ (2003) *Discovering your Personality Type: The Essential Guide to the Enneagram.* Boston: Houghton Mifflin.

Schiff, Aaron and Schiff, Jacqui Lee (1971) Passivity, *Transactional Analysis Journal.*

Schiff, Jacqui Lee (1975) *Cathexis Reader.* New York: Harper and Row.

Searles, H.F. (1955) The informational value of the supervisor's emotional experiences, *Psychiatry,* 18: 135–46 (later reproduced in H.F. Searles, *Collected Papers on Schizophrenia and Related Subjects.* London: Karnac Books, 1965).

Steiner, Claude (1974) *Scripts People Live.* New York: Bantam Books.

Townsend, John (1994) Making messages memorable, *Training and Development,* January.

Index

Made in the USA
Middletown, DE
24 February 2021